WHEN

Good

ISN'T

Good

ENOUGH

The Spiritual Keys To Operating In
The Mindset Of Excellence

RUDOLPH W. MCKISSICK, JR.

WITH FOREWORD BY BISHOP I. V. HILLIARD

ISBN 978-0-9857849-7-3

Library of Congress Cataloging –in-Publication Data:

An application to register this book for Cataloging has been submitted to the Library of Congress. Printed in the USA and Canada.

All Scripture quotations, unless otherwise identified, are taken from the HOLY BIBLE, NEW INTERNATIONAL VERSION®, (NIV)® Copyright © 1973, 1978, 1984 International Bible Society. Used by permission of Zondervan Publishing House. All rights reserved. Scripture quotations marked (KJV) are take from the King James Version. Used by permission of NavPress Publishing Group. All rights reserved. Please note that MarkOne publishing style capitalizes certain pronouns in Scripture that refer to the Father, Son, and Holy Spirit, and may differ from some publishers' styles.

Cover, book, and interior design by KDR Consulting, LLC ®

Published By MarkOne Publishing
3645 Marketplace Blvd, Suite 130-370
Atlanta, Georgia 30344
A subsidiary of KDR Consulting, LLC

DEDICATION

This book is dedicated to my parents,
Bishop Rudolph McKissick, Sr. and Estelle McKissick,
who raised me to always expect the best,
to do the best, and to never settle for anything
beneath the maximum of what I had in potential.
I also posthumously dedicate it to my
father-in-law, Dr. Paul Nichols,
who, as one of my seminary professors,
called me on the carpet in one class,
challenging me to not be satisfied because
I gave a good answer that showed
I had read the material but not a great answer
to show that I understood the material.

It's all about being great and
refusing to be only good enough.

CONTENTS

FOREWORD

My life has been marked by defining moments. As I look back over 50 years of preaching the Gospel, I have seen God intervening in my life on many occasions. A defining moment is a point in time where decisions that are made have life-changing impact. My first defining moment took place in Miss Rachel's house when I gave may heart to Jesus. As a little boy, eating cookies and drinking juice, I sensed that it was my time! Others who were there that day did not realize it, but I did and my life has never been the same.

Another defining moment was when I received the Holy Spirit and all His gifts. I went against the conventional wisdom of the day and received the same power that the early church had. I was no longer operating in my human ability but in the power of God. All of our defining moments are not just spiritual ones. If you are truly looking for more than good enough, you have to be willing to let God take you out of your comfort zone in every area of your life. When you do this, then you will truly be walking by faith.

In your hands, you hold a profoundly important book that will provide a defining moment of revelation that has the potential to transform your life. Bishop Rudolph McKissick is a pastor's pastor and has written a book that calls the Body of Christ to a higher level of living. He, like me, wants to see everyone sitting in our churches, walking in the best God has for their lives. But Bishop McKissick knows that life is choice driven, and if you do not make up your mind to go for more, you will see the promises of God remain on the pages of your Bible.

As I read the book, I could see that this was not another success pie in the sky thesis without Scriptural and practical wisdom but a high level revelation of theological value. It is refreshing to the casual reader and most stimulating to the serious student of faith. This crafty insight into greatness will create a thirst for the next level of living like no other.

If you desire to move from a mediocre effort to a maximized existence, then you will embrace the principles that you read in this book and immediately put them into practice. As you read each chapter, my prayer is that the Holy Spirit will reveal areas in your life where you can step up and take your walk with God to the next level. This book will be the catalyst for a defining moment for you because your power to transform will be long lasting and life changing.

Bishop McKissick is not trying to impress you but help you. Receive this work as such and your days of lack, frustration, and stagnancy will be over. If you are tired of being good enough and are ready for more, then read on!

Maximizing life everyday,
Bishop Bishop I. V. Hilliard
Senior Pastor, New Light Church
Apostle & Presiding Prelate, Association of Independent Ministries

INTRODUCTION

Most parents would feel successful if they raised good children. A business owner feels fortunate to have good employees. 'Good' ensures a quality existence. 'Good' means that all basic needs are met and some extra is left over for a couple of indulgences. We want people to treat us good. We enjoy good food. We pray for good marriages that, with good health, will ensure that we live a good life. 'Good' becomes a way to see the world. 'Good' is how we act and what we believe. 'Good' is a common expectation. 'Good' is a desired outcome. 'Good' is stable. 'Good' is nowhere near 'bad' and two steps past 'Okay'. But, as much as many of us hope for 'Good', I believe we are hindered and even hurt by 'Good'. Why? Because there is another level of quality beyond being and having it good.

'Good' can hold us back. Yes, 'Good' can hold us back! Our desire to be seen as good by others and ourselves often puts us at odds with the radical and dynamic purpose God has placed in us. We care so deeply about how people see us that 'Good' can actually rob us of the greatness God entrusted to us. It can estrange us from excellence, which should be our standard.

For example, maybe you are a good lawyer who wins your share of cases and has garnered a good reputation within the halls of justice but continues to practice law not because it is what you want to do but because it has provided you with a good life. Your heart's desire is to teach children, but you stay in the field you are in because it's not 'Bad' and it's better than 'Okay'. It's actually 'Good'. But in spite of how good it has been for you, there is a tugging in you for something greater. Every day, on your drive to the office, you pass an elementary school. You struggle to find the energy to go to work because your work does not nourish your soul. The longing for what you should be disrupts the superficial joys of clothes, shoes, and nice restaurants, which are the results of your 'Good' life. You keep saying you will teach one day, as 'one day' continues to slip away.

The longing to teach becomes so powerful that you use more and more powerful means to try to suppress the inexhaustible well of divine calling springing in your soul. The struggle of suppressing God's real purpose for your life is literally making you so tired that no matter how many sheep are counted, sleep is as elusive as a shadow. You constantly wonder what people will say when you finally get tired of being good, common, unexceptional, and unmotivated. What will they say when you get tired of wearing a mask of designer make-up to cover your inner frown. You are tired of being 'Good'. You have reached the point where 'Good' is just no longer good enough. You want more. You desire more. You are convinced and convicted that you were made for more.

Here is the challenge of making 'Good' not good enough: 'Good' is seductive. It constantly whispers to us as we strive to leave it behind. 'Good' promises much in comfort and ease but produces just enough to keep you coming back for more. 'Good' allows us to overlook some of the details and still do a respectable job that gets noticed and possibly receives accolades. 'Good' shows that we have gifts but does not mean that we are functioning in our intended purpose or at the level God requires.

This book seeks to be a practical guide to help those who are tired of being 'Good enough' and are ready to take that next step into the greatness that God has destined for them.

Not only is this an introduction to a book, it is an invitation to the higher life. The higher life is about living at a level at which God can optimally utilize our gifts for His glory and to make our lives greater. 'Greater' is not about 'More'; it is about 'Better'. This invitation is for those serious about leaving the past behind and pressing forward. God is constantly inviting us from the maze of being good — or exceptionally mediocre — into an active, passionate life of excellence. Allow these keys of spiritual success to unlock the door of frustration, and allow God's best to change your life. Join me on the journey of discovery where being 'Good' is just no longer good enough.

SEATS AND SERVANTS

I was watching a movie one night, and there was a scene between a father and daughter that had me both smiling and thinking at the same time. This young girl, who thought her father could do anything, asked her father to take her to the moon. The father tried with everything that was in him to explain to her why it would be impossible for him to accomplish that feat. She went away and came back with her own plan. She told her father, "Bring all of the chairs out of the house and stack them on top of each other. You get on the highest one and then hold me up above your head, and I will be able to get to the moon."

As I heard the little girl talking about wanting to get to the moon and crying because she could not get there, it made me think about the many adults who get frustrated because they want to get to the top but just can't get there. It is amazing how many adults think they can manipulate their own success and strategically think they have control or can control elevation. They network with the right people and schmooze in the right circles . . . and still it never takes off.

One thing that alarmed me was when I discovered through reading how many physical diseases come about as a result of our desire to get to the top.

A psychologist by the name of Dr. Alfred Adler, in his book, *The Neurotic Self,* taught that most psychological disorders arise from the striving for power. Many people who are ambitious end up working themselves into sickness while trying to get to the top. He went on to suggest that it is not our occupation that causes sickness or mental disease but rather our intentions. We are transfixed on being superior, on being wealthier, on being prettier, on being more popular, on being more powerful, on being spiritually deeper, and on being the greatest, which does not always translate into being greater.

Consider these thoughts for one moment to prove my point. On any given campus, hundreds of young ladies want to be homecoming queen, but only seven or so will show up to decorate the float. Construction crews are never short of those who want be the foreman, but they have to do a search for people to put up the drywall. Everyone wants to be the greatest, but does that necessarily make you greater?

Jesus said it and the church has forgotten it — if you want to be great, you first have to learn how to serve.

A young lady applying for college had done everything the right way in order to get into any college she desired.

She had a great GPA. She had wonderful SAT scores. As she was filling out an admissions application for the college of her choice, she got stumped by one question when she got to the third page of the application, and that question was: ARE YOU A LEADER?

She had to write with integrity that in her estimation she was not. With that answer, the young lady had decided that the college would not want her, because, in her mind, the question about her leadership capabilities and her calling meant that the college was looking for natural born leaders. Four weeks later, she got a letter in the mail acknowledging her admission into the college and welcoming her into the new freshman class. When she called her admissions counselor, she asked with shock and amazement how in the world she had gotten in when she had admitted that she did not feel she was a born leader. The counselor responded by saying to her that all the other one thousand five hundred applicants said that they were leaders. The counselor then said, "We are accepting you because if everybody is a leader, they need somebody who will follow."

It got me to thinking about what it means to be great and to strive for this greatness. This young lady had decided that being great meant having a certain level of title influence or being in a certain position of power. In reality, the young lady showed us what true greatness and striving for the great life is really all about. BEING GREAT IS ABOUT BEING HUMBLE. How much better off could the Body of Christ be if everybody was not trying to be a leader but was just determined to be great?

The Gospel of Matthew, chapter twenty, beginning at verse twenty, is a perfect example of what being great is not. In that text, we find the mother of the sons of Zebedee making a request that shows that she has a fundamental misunderstanding of what it means to be great. Scholars tell us that this woman is the sister of Mary, which means these are the cousins of Jesus who are named James and John. Mark's version says that this whole thing was in fact their idea and not their mother's. I am not sure which version is correct, and quite frankly, that is not important to the point of the text. She comes to Jesus and asks Jesus if her two sons could occupy the seats on both sides of Jesus in His kingdom. We know that in the context and historicity of the text that she is not referring to Heaven, but in fact, she is pointing to a socio-political kingdom that would overthrow the Roman government and put them as a nation back into power. She is trying to ensure that her sons have such a high position that it would garner greatness for them.

What Jesus responds to her will help us to know that walking in the character of greatness is not something that can be manipulated into or "placed" into by someone greater. Jesus lets the mother and us know what is required first and foremost for the character of greatness to be in your life.

Jesus explains to her that in the economy of His Kingdom, greatness is not defined by a seat but is defined by a spirit, and *that* spirit is the spirit of a servant. They were more interested in seats than they were in servanthood. That is why Jesus goes on to say in the next chapter of Matthew (CF. 23:11) that if you want to be great, you have to have the mindset of servanthood.

This has more modern-day implications than we want to admit. In this self-serving, self-seeking, materialistic culture, we have lost sight of what it truly means to walk in the character of excellence and the spirit of greatness. We live in a day and time where everyone wants a position and the seat that goes with it. Everybody is talking about where they are supposed to sit, but nobody is talking about who they are supposed to serve. As a result of this unfortunate reality, look at what is happening to our world. While we argue over seats, our community is dying. While we argue over seats, injustices are growing. While we argue over seats, voter suppression is on the move. While we argue over seats, gangs are growing and murders are increasing. While we argue over who sits where, our sisters are being castigated in an insecure male-dominated society. While we argue over who sits where, our churches are swelling but not growing. While we pick and choose seats, we have given over the church to entertainment with preachers who parade on television for their own self-centered gains.

Being great and living the character of greatness is more than titles and seats. It's about learning how to serve. Striving for the greater starts by finding the servant in you.

DON'T ALLOW WHO YOU ARE TO BE DETERMINED BY WHERE YOU SIT.

If your sense of "somebodyness" (Yes, I know it is not a word) is determined by being elevated or having a certain seat, then you have allowed the definition of your value and purpose to be relegated to the empowering of a title or position that is given to you by another person. So in a real sense, I turn over the right to name my value to somebody else. That is not being great; that is being bought. What gives you real greatness is the authenticity of personality that is rooted in humility. When you learn to simply be who God created you to be and serve Him out of the authentic nature of who you are, that is when you become great.

A very interesting look at this story in Matthew's Gospel followed by the next story gives us what I believe is the key to greatness. Let's do a comparative analysis of the two stories to see my point.

The next story in Matthew's Gospel finds two men who are blind, while in the previous story there are two men who don't get it concerning power and position . . . blind. When you do a comparison of the two stories, it is my belief that the two blind men represent what greatness looks like and the two sons represent what it does not look like. I know how strange that may seem, given how we define what it means to be great, but come closer with me and hear my comparative analysis of the two stories.

In the story of the two sons, they are concerned about where they will sit. In the story of the two blind men, they sit wherever they can find a seat. The two sons want to be in the seats next to Jesus, while the two blind men just want to be in the space where Jesus is passing by. In the story about the two sons, Jesus asks the question, "WHAT DO YOU WANT ME TO DO FOR YOU?" In next story about two blind men, he asks the very same question, "WHAT DO YOU WANT ME TO DO FOR YOU?"

In the differing answers, we find the key to greatness. In the story about the two sons, they say, "WE WANT SEATS." In the story about the two blind men, they say, "WE WANT SIGHT." Do you get the picture? The two sons want seats in order to be in power with Jesus. The two blind men just want their eyes to be opened so that they can then follow Jesus.

The text ends by saying that they "RECOVERED" their sight. They get back something they had lost. What I believe the church and the people at large need to do is recover our sight. We have lost sight of what it means to be great — lost sight of what it means to have greatness. We keep asking for seats when we ought to be asking for sight, so we can see the least, the last, the lost, and the left out. What we need is sight so we can see the disenfranchised. I don't need a seat. I just want sight so I can serve.

I submit to you that serving and humility is the place where being great begins.

I'M TIRED OF BEING GOOD ENOUGH

M*aximizing Life's Defining Moments* is a thought-provoking book penned by Bishop I.V. Hilliard. In it, he suggests that life is full of defining moments. These defining moments are critical places on which our lives pivot, providing the opportunity for expansion and contraction. These places of definition set the course for our lives. These 'crossroads' of circumstance provide opportunities for our Kingdom commitment to be tested.

Defining moments, Bishop Hilliard suggests, occur to reflect our character, conviction, commitment, and courage. We all have moments of definition, places that press us to ask hard questions of ourselves, and these few and precious moments reveal our progress or lack thereof.

Marriage is a defining moment, a culmination of smaller moments, and leaves an indelible mark on the surface of our lives. Many people make these permanent decisions at critical moments for fleeting reasons, only to later be significantly defined by a miscalculated choice.

Responding to the economic downturn that has cost you the security and satisfaction you once enjoyed is a defining moment. We can become chronically bitter and angry with God for our current status, allowing our faith to sour, or we can positively adapt to this as God's redirection or advancement of our lives. These experiences, and others like them, define us because they place us at a crossroads where our response will ultimately shape and direct our lives. We cannot mismanage these crossroads.

I am convinced that one of the most pivotal and defining moments we all face is not only our response to salvation, but also the resulting decision about the caliber and character of our commitments to Jesus. Simply stated, after choosing to be a disciple of Jesus Christ, what kind of disciple will you be? Saying "I will be a Christian" is a major commitment that carries great significance. The way we live our lives demonstrates the importance of our initial commitment. Being a Christian is important, but if we are not going to be the best we can be, it immediately reflects the importance of Christ to us, or lack thereof. Being a mediocre Christian demonstrates your true commitment and opinion of your faith, as if you are saying that you serve a mediocre God.

Certainly, our God is *not* mediocre! Sadly, our stewardship of the gifts and resources that we have been given suggests a different reality. Too many people are arrested by their apathy and are in bondage to their behavior. When we find ourselves living lives of defeat and delay, we have not lived up to God's investment. By setting our goals to the level of 'just enough' and 'easy street', our consistent and fervent spring of ability becomes dammed by our lack of discipline and focus.

Our God is not receiving the most from us, because we are actively blocking our blessings. This focused effort to be mediocre becomes a daily struggle, which, if we are not careful, we turn into a lifestyle. Laziness, apathy, and self-doubt lower our ability to become all that God desires. God becomes smaller, in our estimation, because we have enlarged smaller gods, thereby positioning them as the comfort of our inactive and underproductive lifestyle. There is great superficial benefit to being comfortable. We all desire a measure of security and peace of mind. The problem arises when we try to use comfort to insulate ourselves from the constant pressure that our talents and gifts demand of us. Hiding in the comfort of your job does not make the still, small voice of God quieter. It's ineffective when God asks you to leave your job and start your own business. Owning the trappings of success does not erase the vision that God has truly placed in your heart.

You may have to let go of the 'toys' in your life, because playtime is over. Many of us have become slaves to our comfort and constantly find ourselves in prisons of pillows, which we are constantly fighting to get out of.

Although comfort can often place us in a holding pattern of life, doubt is also a harsh reality. Many of us lack the self-confidence to truly believe we can accomplish what God has revealed. We may have supreme belief in God's power but no faith in our own. If belief in God were all you needed, we would all have more access to what God has assigned for our lives. But the sober truth is that we must have faith in God *and* in ourselves, or we cannot live the abundant life that He has designed for us. Even if you see no good in yourself, you must do it for God's sake and your own. God is working through you, and no matter what you have done or where you have been, God is always willing and able to restore and develop a confidence in you that will empower your efforts.

We, as individuals, have become too comfortable in the quicksand of 'average', so we must choose to become better, more, and greater than 'good enough'. We must walk away from being merely good enough.

It is a hard, lonely walk for many of us. The only thing we have known is an unfulfilled life of wishing and wanting. Because so many people are in this place, we have a community of under-achievers, so much so that mediocrity is in every facet of our society. Consistent and persistent mediocrity in the way we serve one another, and the art of making excuses for our negligence without much reflection, have both become standard practice.

I clearly recognize that if mediocrity, excessive compromise, and underachievement are in every area of society, then it is even more damaging in the church. Many churches are arrested and ensnared by the spirit of comfortable mediocrity. The rituals, traditions, and structures of the church have too often become tools to ensure that mediocrity reigns supreme. Surely the church of the Lord Jesus would desire to be the very best by embracing the people they are working so hard to exclude. The young, the un-churched, populations of non-European descent, and those of the Hip-Hop culture have been ignored because the saints fell asleep behind the wheel of progress. The Lord is calling us to a higher standard because we have been commissioned to live a greater life, with greater influence and impact.

I believe that walking away from mediocrity and 'good enough' may be a lonely and difficult journey. It may mean that the gifts that have always gotten you out of problems may not be able to rescue you in this season. It will mean making the decision to turn your back on a worldly, comfortable path of aimlessness, to trust God and your ability to be what God intended. This may demand that your familiar friends must change. It may mean that you have to move to a new place to live, or even be forced to realize that one of your deepest fears is real, which, for many, is not a fear of being obscure but of being the center of attention.

We must choose to walk away from 'good enough'. We must decide that we will be better spouses than we were before, exhibit more integrity in our business dealings, and become more diligent in our work habits. God is calling us to greater works!

In John 14, Jesus teaches His disciples about the mysterious power that drives His Earthly ministry. Jesus, being fully human and fully divine, speaks of the power present through the indwelling of the Spirit. Jesus teaches us that He is the way to the Father. He is the visible, tangible, manifested image of the Father. He is the manifestation of the Godhead in a bodily form. Because of Jesus' humanity, He had to be empowered beyond human means to accomplish the great feats by which His ministry is most defined.

Jesus' basic principle states that God is in Christ; therefore, Christ is able to do great things. So, because Christ dwells in us, that same power to do great things resides in us. And Jesus says not only great things but ". . . greater things than these . . ." (John 14:12).

What are these 'greater things'? Jesus healed the sick, raised the dead, gave sight to the blind, and multiplied material resources. He met people's spiritual and physical needs because He was being maximized by God's power. In turn, Jesus says that because of His indwelling, we can do greater things than He did in his Earthly body. We are called to be greater because we have been filled with 'greater' by the greatest power in the universe. Because I have been empowered for greater living, I cannot and must not settle for 'good enough'!

We should be like Jesus, but, admittedly, we cannot do everything Jesus did. Do not go down to the funeral home and lay hands on someone's casket and think that they will get up from the dead. Do not try to cater your family reunion by breaking five pieces of Wonder Bread and two pieces of tilapia. I'm being humorous, but we cannot do all Jesus did. However, He said that we could do greater things than He did in the body.

When we let the Holy Spirit maximize the power in us through gifts and abilities given by God, we can have a more expansive impact than a first-century Jesus in Palestine.

Furthermore, we are called to go to the ends of the Earth, and when we are empowered by the Holy Spirit for Kingdom work, God will extend our capacity beyond anything we can imagine! Because He has called us into a greater destiny of living, do not make the mistake of missing 'greater'. The desire to walk behind the seduction of 'good' can easily force you to miss your designed greater living.

You are meant for more — for greater. We are created to expand! I believe that many people have lived life at such a compromised and at a defeated level that to them a greater *anything* seems like a foreign concept. It's hard to see past this moment, but God has designated and appointed each one of us for greater! Regardless of all the excuses and failures that we try to offer in exchange for lower standards and expectations, God still empowers us for excellence and greater capacity, whether we understand it or not.

Some of us have a permanent gray cloud of defeat hanging over us like a personal tornado, constantly destroying any thought or momentum that points us to a greater life. We keep negative people around, who quickly tell us that our lack of education, access, and resources will constantly keep us out. When they constantly belittle our dreams and defuse our moment, they're hard at work to be discouraging.

Lift up your head and increase your expectation! God is calling us and demanding that we be better than good; instead, we must do greater.

Here is the sad reality. Many believers are not in danger of ruining their lives but of something far worse — *wasting* their lives! Ruining our lives means we are active in its affairs and have made a mistake. The alternative is far worse, because we allowed the fruit of our talent to die on the vine. We lack the ability to discern the value of our gift and live as if our lives do not matter, when, in fact, they are precious treasures. I have heard it said that the places with the most collective potential are graveyards. Do not waste what you were given. Get active and commit to greater living!

Though it sounds simple, we cannot just walk casually into 'greater'. It costs something. 'Greater' requires a sacrifice. Greater living means greater accountability, responsibility, and commitment. Simply stated, we refuse to walk into greater character because character costs. Being a consistent and powerful tool for God does not obscure my character. It means that I must struggle and sacrifice to have the solid life that 'greater' can be built upon.

My heart is aching for those who are stuck in the starting blocks of life, in the back of the line of progress. You know you were meant for more but have settled for less. You have tried to fill your hunger with crumbs, but you know that the rumbling will not stop. I want to inspire those who have been knocked down one time too many or those who have seen the worst of life and feel as if they are captive to the past. I am screaming at you through this book! You are called for greater works!

I have also come with a spiritual alarm clock for the lazy and the sluggish. The dreamland of imagination is over. God will not allow your talent to waste away under the guise of

24

I'M TIRED OF BEING GOOD ENOUGH

activity when you have not even broken a sweat on any one effort or idea. Wake up and go get greater! It is time to live!

It costs to be greater. It means that I must honestly bare my soul for self-examination.

Breast cancer is one of the most potent and persistent diseases with which we contend. There are many things that we can do to try to avoid breast cancer, but it is not completely preventable. The best method of detection and first line of defense is self-examination, feeling for any bumps, knots, or irregularities as a means of critical detection at an early stage. This self-exam saves many lives, because detection and self-examination helps to properly treat the problem at a smaller juncture.

In similar fashion, we must examine ourselves to see if we have been living below God's calling and standard. Like a breast exam, it is a needed checkup. Some people will allow the embarrassment of self-examination to rob them of the full life God has intended. The lack of transparency with oneself in private can ultimately cost one the opportunity to become greater and do greater things in public.

Specialists in the medical field understand that many people will struggle with administering a self-test, so they also suggest that their spouse or intimate partner administer the test. Allowing someone you love to administer a sensitive and private test helps to ease the fears and embarrassment found internally. Some of us have fallen out with friends and family because they will not be party to our complacency and underachievement. Examine yourself and allow others to examine you to prevent your gifts from dying on the vine. Jesus said we can do ". . . greater works than these . . ." and we must do that!

The call to be good is sweet, but the calling to a greater life is bigger than you and your circumstances. 'Greater' means that our preconceived boundaries are no longer an issue.

Then the question arises, "What will we do now?"

I remember hearing a story about a dog that lived in a fenced back yard for many years. The dog desired to run free down the street with the other dogs. One day, a storm came and knocked down a section of the fence. The dog walked to the place where the fence once stood and sat, unable to run free even though the fence was no longer there. He had become conditioned by the barrier to believe that going beyond the barrier was impossible, even when the visible barrier had been moved. It was no longer seen by his eyes, but was seen in his mind. Likewise, Jesus has removed the barrier of being 'good' for us and now presents the opportunity for a life beyond your wildest dreams. The reality is that too many never reach the level of 'greater' or 'excellent' because they have allowed their expectations and dreams to be defined and hindered by a fence that has already been removed.

We cannot consistently function in the 'gap' between what we are and what we can be. This intermediate place of discomfort means that we must make some major decisions about who we are and what we are doing.

I trust God. His promises are sure, so if I am not living a 'greater works' life, it must be my fault. Typically, this disjointed approach is a character issue and a crack in the foundation of our lives.

"Greater is the place where you begin to understand, by faith, that God is ready to accomplish something through you that is normally beyond human reach and ability." This is where we begin to understand the fuller extent of greater works. We have to allow God the space and be the yielded vessel to do things through us that are seemingly unachievable. God is ready and simply waiting on us to decide to be serious enough about His will and His Word that we will allow Him to fully operate over our lives. You and I must embrace an encounter with the infinite God and become a flowing river of His power.

God's power is actively transforming you beyond what you see in yourself on your best day. God is saying, "When I do My thing in and through you, it will be more productive and influential than your best day!" 'Greater' is what God sees in us before we can even conceive of our 'greater'. It's beyond what we can imagine. Yet this is what God has seen in us the entire time. God looks at us through the eyes of greater works, not 'good enough'. We do not serve a 'good enough' God! We serve a God who wastes no time but invests in each of us with an expectation for greater works.

I have given spiritual advisement to people for many years, and I am aware of the deep-seated mentality of being and doing only 'good enough'. 'Leaving well good enough alone' is illustrated more clearly in Genesis 11:31-32. Canaan was the divine destination from the beginning of the journey of Terah. Terah and his family left the Ur of the Chaldeans and began to head to Canaan. They came to live in Heron, a big city known for its marina and nice ships and thriving economic environment. It was similar to how New York City would seem to a man from a small country town. It is almost as if you were leaving *Green Acres* and moving to a city that you have heard of but have never seen.

Terah, Abraham's father, died in Haran, a place of 'good enough'. He stopped short and missed out because he settled for the suitable, and because the suitable felt good, he skipped 'greater'. I hope we realize that we will 'die' like Terah if we continue to do good enough. Our marriages will die if we do not do more than good enough. Our churches will die if we can only muster a good enough response to the needs of the world. Your dreams will die if you keep smothering the life out of them. This world will die if we continue in our 'good enough' ways.

I believe that when you decide to just be good enough, you will end up in comfortable complacency — comfortable just getting by. This 'just getting by' mentality will then lead to miserable mediocrity. Knowing that we try to live at the level of 'good enough' places us in a situation where we struggle against our own future, and it leaves us exhausted and unfulfilled. The mediocrity that we wallow in will ultimately erode the core of who we are. By allowing 'good enough' to control us, we lose the freedom to become what God intended. In this situation, God is not in control; we are. We are the cause and cure of much of our stagnation and frustration. Because the choice is ours, we must refuse to submit to the unyielding taskmaster of 'average' that seeks to controls us.

'Average' or 'good enough' restricts advancement and stifles creativity. It demoralizes our ability and our desire to take risks and embrace new things. Sadly, 'good enough' is a sign of being lukewarm. John tells us in the book of Revelation that Jesus spits a lukewarm church out of His mouth, so surely our lukewarm efforts at marriage, school, family relationships, and faith-life would not escape Christ's inspection.

Another danger of 'good enough' is that it looks okay from the outside. A job looks good enough because you work for a reputable establishment and make a good salary. A relationship looks good enough from the outside because you both seem to have so much going for yourselves.

The shiny exterior of 'good enough' hides a serious secret, that in your inner reality, the unfulfilled part of you will scream until it dies, because 'good enough' is never enough. 'Good enough' is comparable to eating candy all day, every day. Though we are consuming the calories our bodies need in order to live, the candy does not nourish us. We will soon be alive but unfulfilled and sickly. 'Good enough' keeps us active but does not benefit us. It fills but does not satisfy. 'Good enough' seems like enough but is only a façade.

Although 'good enough' seems beneficial, it is not where God called us to be. Living below God's 'best' places puts each of us in a position to exhibit baseline living. When we stay in things God did not lead us into or engage us in, or things that God did not desire, we live below our God-ordained purpose.

So, in order to break out of mediocrity, we must wage war on the enemy. We must break out of doing just enough to get by, fit in, and blend in with things that detract from us. We have to break out of ways that rob us of the 'greater' that Jesus spoke upon us. We must confront the enemy.

Here comes the challenge of that confrontation: In many instances, that enemy is the 'inner self'. You cannot continue to blame the economy, the System, the Man, your past, or anything that *happened to you* for your baseline living. It is not the fault of the T-ball coach when you were five years old who would not let you play. Sometimes we have to look in the mirror of self-reflection and confront the enemy that resides inside us. We cannot give others power over us by blaming them for our actions. The faster we take responsibility for the current condition of our lives, the faster we can maximize this season and do greater works for God.

I believe that it is therapeutic to look yourself in the mirror and address the issues you have. When we can say, "I am the one," we regain a sense of purpose and empowerment, because we do not have to blame anyone anymore for why we are where we are. Learn to inspect yourself and, if necessary, make some hard confessions:

"I am the one who keeps breaking my word."

"I am the one who stops me from being a better business owner."

"I am the one who keeps sabotaging my relationships."

"I am the one who gossips about other people."

"I am the one who cannot be trusted."

"I am the one who does not tell the truth."

You and I must name our issues and confront our inner selves so that we can remedy them. Stop blaming people for your problems when the prescription is in your pocket. Confront the enemy and gain the victory.

Laziness is the biggest robber of talent and the thief of purpose. Laziness becomes a self-created womb to protect a person from the responsibilities of the outside world. Being lazy is a way for the enemy to attempt to control us; it makes us think we will do everything we are created to do . . . *later.* Pushing the start date back for our greater life only delays our progression, and while we recline, time passes quickly and night will soon come. At that point, no man can work. Laziness is the parking brake to your advancement. Laziness and self-doubt are equally effective. Understand that laziness and 'greater' are not compatible for the maximized Christian life.

The good news is that we are better than what we have become. We are better than what has happened to us or what we have done. We are more than what we are accused of being. Often, we do not believe this because we do not allow ourselves to realize that God is much greater than we are willing to engage. God's greatness seeks to be manifested through us, and we will not have peace until we allow ourselves the unrestricted ability to trust God and allow ourselves to be greater.

When we decide to leave 'good' behind and become greater, it puts us in a position where impossibilities cannot coexist with God's promises. The promises of God make the impossible possible. God's assurance makes the seemingly impossible an absolute certainty. Many of us are intimidated because God has shown us something about our lives that is larger than we can imagine and more expansive than we can plan. We often allow the size of the vision to determine our level of belief or unbelief. It then seems impossible. You do not know how you will ever reconcile with that child you disowned or get married after the age of forty, but beloved, what seems and feels impossible with humans is certainly a possibility with God.

This kind of belief is rooted in a solid belief in God's Word. We have to depend on His Word and trust it like our next breath depends on it. God's Word is true and sure. We have to cling to the certainty of His Word even when the circumstances are not favorable and the winds are not fortuitous. Things can look bad and may even *be* bad, but His assurances that the water will not overtake you and that your enemies will not triumph over you are where we must stand. This seems impossible, but God seeks to do greater through us. For that to happen, we must often submit our reality to His promises and push past the barriers.

Because Jesus has declared, "Greater is He that is in me," I can be greater than my best victory. I can be greater than the worst moment of my life. I can be greater than the abuse I survived. I can be greater than the disappointment of my childhood. I can be greater than the abandonment I feel. God is calling me to a higher plane, a place of 'greater' that eyes have not seen and ears have not heard. I want you to want greater for your life!

I declare to you that even as you are reading these words, 'greater' is coming for you! Not a greater house or car or salary, but a greater you! God wants you to be a greater you. The world is waiting for the emergence of your 'greater'. Why would God give greater resources to a person who does not want to be greater? Why would God grant more to the person who rejects the responsibility of having more? God is seeking to express divine greatness in the Earth, but we cannot be conduits of power if we do not allow it to flow through us.

I want to encourage you to not become or remain scared of what it will take to be you. You must know that you are supposed to change the world. You were born to change the world. Don't hide beneath the baggage, like Saul, or settle for the suitable, like Terah. Don't hide or settle because you are afraid of having to dress differently, change friends, or go back to school. You know who you are supposed to be, but the steps to become that person will require a higher level of sacrifice and commitment. We hide from the steps of progression, but we are also hiding from the 'greater' that God has shown us. We have to embrace what it takes to be who we are and live confidently in God's power.

Jesus realized that we would need to confront the seductive power of being good enough. The desire to be good enough is always present, but the power to be greater is waiting for us to simply believe and receive it. As you read this book, I challenge you to reach up and grab beyond the good enough that seems to satisfy you.

I'M LEAVING GOOD ENOUGH ALONE

lisha is one of the most interesting characters in the biblical narrative. Although he is a mighty man in his own right, many people get him confused with Elijah, and think that they just have the pronunciation and spelling of his name wrong. Others do not pay much attention to him because of the magnitude of familiarity they have with his predecessor, Elijah. Imagine being great but being overshadowed by someone who is also great. Better yet, imagine being called to a level of greatness by someone who is always on that level and the challenge that comes with trying to meet or match what they have been able to do. I know that feeling all too well in sharing in ministry with my father, a man who has walked in excellence from day one.

My look at the life and transition from Elijah to Elisha was birthed out of my own personal struggles with ministry and transition from my "Elijah" (My incredible father). My struggle birthed a series of sermons where I saw myself as Elisha who needed to break away from just being good enough. While we will see Elisha's transition being going from one place or leaving one place to another, mine was leaving a mindset.

Elisha came on the scene right after the mental breakdown of Elijah as a result of his battle on Mt. Carmel with the prophets of Baal and the ensuing threat made on his life by Jezebel. I chose to highlight this individual and circumstance to make a simple but powerful point. As God began to put Elijah back on his feet, Elijah had a 'pity party' conversation with God. One of the last things he said to God is that he felt all alone in fighting for the things of God. He was in an emotionally fatigued and depressed position, experiencing the sum of all fears; he felt alone and confused, and his life seemed meaningless.

Elijah was suffering from depression so deep that death's inviting arms seemed an ideal place to retire after a life of doing God's work. This is important to discuss, because mental health is a crucial area that many churches avoid. It is interesting to think about mental health in this way: If we sprained an ankle or broke a finger, we would go to a doctor. If our mind is strained and stressed, we see that as a sign of weakness. This stigma attached to mental health places many people, especially pastors and leaders, in isolated positions, ready to be ambushed. Too many pastors and leaders are suicidal, and some even moving forward with the act because they, like Elijah, got alone with their own thoughts and saw no hope of rescue in sight. The mental health of leaders is something that deserves more attention that I am giving in these small thoughts. It is my hope that we will begin to see as leaders that counseling is a necessity to a healthy mental state when in leadership.

Elijah left his servant in Judah and walked on alone until he got up under a juniper tree and there began his suicide diatribe. Watching channels like Animal Planet and other nature-based programming teaches us that predators target the young, old, and injured. If an injured zebra becomes isolated from the group, death is looming. The enemy seeks to isolate those mentally distressed from the community and fellowship of believers for a strategic attack. No matter who you are or where you are from, do not allow the enemy to isolate or shame you because of depression or mental anguish. You are not weak. Seek and obtain your healing!

Elijah wanted to die. He wanted his life to end. This is not simply isolated to Elijah's day and time. Suicide is running rampant in our world because hopelessness and isolation are standard practice in human relationships. We read sad stories of those whose mental affliction or situational problem overwhelm them to the point of prematurely ending their life. It may seem farfetched, but pastors and leaders have allowed life to escape through their feeble fingers because their grip on the world was unsure and slipping quickly. Where does the counselor go to get counseling? Who does the shepherd confide in? Elijah was on dangerous ground, but God offered him an option that preserved his life and extended his legacy.

The enemy has tried that trick in my own life. Pastoring, preaching, fathering, and being a spouse, a son, and a friend had me at wit's end. In theory, it would have been easier to quit and run away, but I knew that the enemy wanted to get me to leave my blessed position. The only way the enemy could think of to move me out my position was to make me loathe my life and block my vision of who I would become. Like Elijah, I made the mistake of keeping my frustration to myself and sitting up under my juniper tree with my own thoughts and dysfunctional self-talk. I realized that the Devil is a liar. I have the victory in Jesus and I have people who love me. Count your blessings and never discount how much the enemy wants you to get off your spot and out of the way.

God, sensing Elijah's frustration, instructed him to anoint three different people: Hazael, as King of Aram; Jehu, as King of Israel; and Elisha, as his successor. Please don't miss the point in this simple instruction from God: Elijah said there was nobody else on his side. God said, "Listen, just because you don't know whom I have in mind does not mean there is nobody else out there on My side." God has people out here of whom you are not aware, whom He is preparing to place into His purpose. Just because you think you are alone does not mean that you are alone. Contrary to popular thought, when you walk and live by faith, you can't always allow perception to be reality.

God never does anything off the cuff, which means God already had Elisha selected before Elijah knew it. It was always on God's mind to anoint Elisha. You must realize that God already had Elisha on His mind before Elisha or Elijah knew anything about it. That is a powerful word for everyone:

God has you on His mind for an assignment long before you will ever know that you were even on His mind. Just because we are not mindful of our purpose or know the plans of God, we cannot underestimate how much God has planned for us. God called us before the world was formed to be who we are. God has us in mind down to the number of hair follicles on our heads and in our sinks. God is not making this up as He goes along. God knows what your gifts are and seeks to guide you into greater use of those gifts.

God knows your strengths and your shortcomings. Your problems, propensities and proclivities are not new to God. Your problems do not surprise God. He called us and placed us in the center of His Will long before we knew about it or Him. The Bible lets us know, "While we were yet sinners, Christ died for us." There is no surprising God! He saw you coming and already has a place for you.

Now watch where Elisha is when God gives the instruction: He is in the field, plowing. He is not a sage or a prophet in training. As a matter of fact, we see no evidence that he is holy. He is a stable and successful business owner, but not the heir apparent to the prophetic mantle of Israel. I know you may not like where you are right now, and where you are may seem distant from where you think you should be. Nevertheless, take courage in knowing that God already has you in mind and in His plans. Keep working and being faithful in what you know to do so you can become all God intends for you.

Remain faithful to where you are, because God is already behind the scenes of your life, preparing your future and your destiny. Elisha had no idea of the breakthrough that was about to happen in his life. His life was going to be revolutionized instantly. He was about to be an 'overnight celebrity'. His future flight into greatness was already booked; the prophetic plane was about to take off. God was talking to Elijah about Elisha. It may sound odd, but God is talking about you behind your back! Whenever God talks about you behind your back, He is getting ready to demonstrate something through your life.

God has been talking about you to your boss; a friend is hooking you up with a great person or arousing favor in the heart of the bank officer. God is speaking about you to others in order to prepare a blessing for you that is bigger than yourself. Folks, wisdom suggests that when you are being talked about, your ears will burn. Maybe what you are really feeling are your spiritual ears burning as God talks about you to people who can take your life to the next level.

God is present with you, watching over you and planning great things for you. Can I tell you what else this means? Do not be fooled by who a person is because of where they are in life right now. Elisha was doing a dirty, stinky, filthy job, but he had an anointing for greatness on his life. Don't judge people by where you find them. Just because they don't have the pedigree, haven't been in the right social circles, or have never met the right people, doesn't mean anything to God. God can take you from the worst of the worst and make you the best of the best. That's what He did for Elisha, and He can do it for you too. He is in the process of doing it for somebody else right now. Listen to me, your current condition is never an indication of your future potential. Did you hear what I just said? Your future potential is never defined by or determined by your current condition and state in life.

Now, if you can't judge people by where you find them, then you should not judge yourself by where you currently are. Too many people bring destiny indictments on themselves because of their current status or condition. You start to settle into where you are and convince yourself that you ought to be grateful, thereby allowing your gratitude to lead to satisfaction. Now, don't get me wrong; you ought to be grateful, but when I know that God has made me for more, I will not allow gratitude for a pit stop in life to lull me into satisfaction. The Apostle Paul said in Philippians 4:11, "I have learned to be content in whatsoever state I find myself". Content does not mean complacent. It means that if this is where God has me then I will not complain about it but will learn from it. That does not mean that I resign to be stuck in it when I know it is beneath my potential and purpose God has for my life.

I will work on myself wherever God places me, so that when He is ready to move me, I am ready to be moved. Scripture declares that in spite of what Elisha was involved in, when the call for 'greater' came, he had no problem walking away from a 'good enough' life. This is the critical juncture for Elisha. The average person, and I do mean *average,* would resist change, even if it was positive. Can you walk away from 'good enough'?

That is the question at the crux of this book.

A good life is the enemy of the God life. Elisha is pinched by the prospect of purpose. He cannot stay the same. He cannot allow good to keep him from God. We want a suburban house or a downtown loft. We have high hopes for success and making the most of our gifts. If you had one chance, in a brief moment in time, to be what God has designed for you, would you be able to do it? Many of us give sufficient lip service to walking away from everything, but few would do it. I believe God may be tapping people on the proverbial shoulder through this book to see if they are ready for their life to change. God is calling us into deeper fellowship and relationship, manifested in response to the moment of God's call for a deeper life. When God knocks at your door of change, will you be home to answer?

Another principle for practical living is that *we should not allow stability to become a stumbling block.* The day Elisha receives the call from God through the prophet, he is doing what he does every day — the ordinary. Wake up, get dressed, get the plow, drive the oxen, eat lunch, drive the oxen, get clean, get dinner, go to bed, and then wake up the next morning to start all over again. It was good, hard work. It is believed that Elisha was in charge of teams of oxen owned by a wealthy landowner, or he could have owned his own business. He had a good job. It gave him stability.

Stability is a noble goal for most people. Many, especially those in the midst of troubling economic times, would love the stability Elisha had. Stability can become a stumbling block when it deadens your sensibilities to a higher calling and purpose in God through Christ Jesus. You may be stable in a relationship that is good but not God's best. I have heard it said, "Half a shoe is better than no shoe at all." That makes sense in terms of being barefoot but not in a relationship with another person. It is not about using someone as a stable placemat, holding a position until something better comes along. We can be rocked to sleep in a stable relationship that is going absolutely nowhere. We will not leave because we are so stable that we become mummified by a lack of movement. This is not just a principle for relationships but for job, friendships, ministry and any other are of life where things are good and stable.

Don't let your routine become a distraction to revelation. Routine becomes the driving force of stability. Don't get me wrong; routine can be good and is a needed part of a balanced and prepared existence. The danger in the maintenance of routine is that if you stay there long enough, you can become dependent on the routine. Then you become afraid to leave the routine, even though you actually *hate* the routine. When God is calling you out of the good enough life and into a higher life it means that God is calling you out of the routine. My warning to you is don't get so used to it and dependent upon it that you can't even trust God enough to cut you from it and lead you to 'greater'. You can become so busy plowing that you get scared to leave it to walk in purpose. So now you settle for suitability and succumb to mediocrity.

Maybe you are pastoring, and the routine of ministry is lulling you to sleep. Sundays are considered narcoleptic worship experiences. The Christian Education department is still teaching from the same books as forty year ago. The choir sings the same songs. The sermons sound the same. The routine has been helpful to provide cohesion but has created a stiff sense of form. The ministry functions are doing just enough to be active but not enough to be excellent. The members refuse to go beyond mere Sunday attendance. Do not let routine keep you from realizing what God is doing outside of your routine. Go back to school. Attend conferences on ministry. Take your staff to leadership conferences.

There is so much that happens outside of our daily routines. The world is so big, and many of our routines keep us from seeing the newness of what God has for us. God is always seeking to show us more than we have seen and take us far beyond our well-meaning desires for normalcy. There is more to life than reality TV and running the streets. God wants to take us higher, but many of us have fallen in love with the ground. There is nothing too hard for God, but we must be open to how God speaks to us in order for us to amend our routines and enlarge our circles.

Elijah, the dejected prophet of Yahweh, has found his help in Elisha. How did he cement this transition of prophetic power and break the cycle of routine, stable and good enough in his protégé? Elijah placed a cloak on Elisha. A cloak is not as common now as it was in the ancient Middle East. During the biblical day it meant a great deal. A cloak was one of the most important items of clothing a person could own. It would protect the wearer from storms and bad weather by providing cover and warmth. Elisha was being given something to represent what God was doing in his life. Elisha was being called from the ordinary to the extraordinary and would need covering for the many days he would have to walk alone, exposed to the elements. The cloak would be a barrier between the outer storms and an inner calm. Elijah puts the cloak around Elisha to signify that God will cover him wherever he goes and protect him from the raging storms of life.

God wants to shift you from ordinary to extraordinary by giving you something that will not make sense for where you are but will help you get where you are going. The cloak did not mean much to Elisha the plowman, but it signaled a power awakening as Elisha the prophet. God will give you things to protect you from the problems that you will face.

The cloak was also for bedding, to provide a place to rest, and it allowed Elisha to be at home in the most adverse situations. Elijah's life consisted of traveling and moving in and out of various contexts. He was able to navigate those different spaces, in part, because the cloak would allow him to rest anywhere. It kept him close to rest and security. We cannot always go to comfortable places, but God will equip us to be comfortable wherever we are. God will provide you with what you need so that your comfort is not dependent on context. Elisha was equipped with a material garment that reminded him of the rest that God provides in the midst of pressure.

Cloaks are interesting, especially for one last reason: It was a solemn promise between Elijah and Elisha. The promise of the cloak was basically saying, "I declare in the 'right now' about what shall be done in the 'not yet'." To a New Testament believer that sounds less like a cloak and more like a statement of faith. When you walk by faith in the promises of God you should be able to utter those same words about yourself and your life.

Elijah says nothing to Elisha about becoming the new prophet. Notice that the solemn promise did not articulate that Elisha would be Elijah's successor. At that time, he was just an assistant — to the premier prophet in the land. He was leaving everything he had on a pledge. *The promise of what he would be was greater than who he thought he would be.*

I hope to challenge you to see what God is calling you to do. This book is for those who are actively seeking to leave the ordinary. Maybe you feel flustered and frustrated because you know God has great things in store for you but it hasn't happened. You see that your routine is being broken up and that God is introducing you to the greater life. It may feel daunting and even depressing to be bound by routine and the ordinary, but when God puts your destiny around your shoulders, you'll know that everything is going to change.

Elisha's future is brighter because God had him in mind. Our future should be brighter because God has use for us. I don't know about you, but I am ready to embrace the greater life. God provides a mantle or cloak for everyone who seeks to be great. That covering does not seem to make sense because we cannot judge our future selves from within our present condition. God keeps people expectant and excited about what's new. Allow God to take you to the next level and blow your mind, but it all starts with a choice to forsake the ordinary for an extraordinary life serving God with no limits on your future.

SURRENDER
YOUR PLOW

As a youngster, I needed to learn how to swim. Desiring to do well, I monitored my progress the entire summer of swimming at the Johnson Family YMCA. I believe in working hard, because it is often said that hard work ensures a more successful outcome. I had learned how to paddle, cup my hands, and hold my breath. I took great care and concern in mastering the finer points. I had all the aesthetics and movements down. I looked like a swimmer!

Although I looked successful, I encountered a problem during the last test. They quietly led us to the deep end of the pool for this final test. In order to complete this level and rise to the next, which was receiving our certificate as swimmers, we had to jump off the diving board and into the pool. This may seem monotonous and uneventful for those who are at home in the water, but for many, including myself, this represented the sum of all evils.

As fear caused my heart to flutter, I realized that an alert and engaged lifeguard loomed on the edge of the pool, ready and eager to assist us after we jumped into what we little boys saw as the mysterious deep end of an ocean. I was petrified and terrified. The director of the YMCA at that time was a gentleman by the name of Mr. Lawrence Jones (who now happens to be the Chairperson of MY Trustee Ministry at the church SMH). Mr. Jones was an ever-present reminder of my parents' wishes for me to become a swimmer. Eventually, Mr. Jones came out to the pool, and seeing my hesitancy, he told me, "Jump in or I'll jump on you!" I can hear you laughing right now.

I am a great swimmer now, but to this very day I refuse to jump off a diving board because I am still traumatized by that event. The scary and ironic part of my minor diving fear was not that it was in the deep end of the pool. I have seen people navigate deep water, and I routinely swam in nine feet of water without hesitation. I was not fearful of the teacher. I did not fear embarrassment in front of my classmates. I did not have issues with my body or concerns about my ability to perform the swimming aspect of the test. The scariest aspect of that entire swimming test — that scary moment of evaluation of my current skill set and potential elevation to a new level — was diving into the pool. Here is what I mean. Diving is not merely jumping into a pool. Rules at a pool will generally dissuade people from diving into the shallow end, which can be dangerous. People normally jump into shallow water feet first because they can readily find the bottom and land safely. Jumping allows some level of control but is a limited risk; it allows a person to change their location by using their force to push against the ground to shift where they have been. Shallow water, like many not-deep things in life, requires a jump . . . not a dive.

Things that are not deep are not necessarily trivial or unimportant. On the contrary, we have to jump into things that are important but are not core convictions. We jump into roles, relationships, and situations, knowing that our involvement only requires a limited engagement. We are still in relative control, but by leaping we have taken a risk. We jump into a situation to provide help to someone, knowing that it is only temporary. Life often brings us face to face with situations that are like jumping into shallow water.

Notice that jumping into the shallow end was not the test. I was not given a passing mark because I could navigate the shallow end with a feeble jump. The test was designed for us to dive into the deep water. I had to relinquish my belief in my control of the situation, jump into the air, and dive into the water. I could do my part, but the heights I was diving from and the depths that I faced created more uncertainty than I could imagine. I had to relinquish my belief that I could control my destiny.

Passing this test was not about being able to swim. I had demonstrated that I could swim. Being able to swim was what had brought me to that point. It was not about conquering an amount of water that was over my head; I had done that. This test was about my willingness to surrender to and trust the person in the pool. Passing this test was not about swimming; it was about surrendering. I had to give up to go up. When I let go was when I was able to go to the next level.

Surrendering seems like a foreign concept to grasp. We live in a world that tells us that we must gain control, keep control, and control the control we have worked so hard to obtain. Surrendering seems counterintuitive, almost like giving up. I recognize that as an American, we like winners. We love people who never give up. Giving up is treated like a character flaw, an unpardonable sin of the will. Nobody likes a quitter, and surrendering smells too much like quitting.

Surrendering is not quitting. Surrendering, in reference to my swimming test, was not giving up. Giving up was as simple as climbing down the ladder and going home. I did not learn defeat; I learned how to surrender. Surrender is not about admitting defeat. Surrender is not about a critical weakness of character. Surrender is about trusting God's providence, care, and plan enough to lean on the invisible promises, even when the material manifestation is not obvious. The promise was not that everything would be perfect. The promise, as signaled by the lifeguard's presence, was that I would have all the support I needed, and, because I was at the diving board, he believed I would succeed. I surrendered that moment to God and did my thing!

Interestingly, full surrender to God's plan often feels like losing control. That is because you are losing control of your myth of control. Our believed control is one of the main causes of anxiety and stress. Believing that we should be in full control is a deceptive belief that tricks us into thinking we're God. Our manic need for control and order, especially when it involves controlling people, is a major source of family struggle, mental frustration, and spiritual unease.

We were endowed with limited capacity, but we think we are infinitely wise. Our desire to control affairs, situations, and people actually controls us. The constant pressure of staying in control is controlling even the person who believes they are in control. It is a cycle of oppression. Surrender breaks the cycle of control and opens new ways of living. Surrender is not weakness. Surrender is actually strength. Surrender is a journey.

The upgrade to the greater life is a journey. It is not something you simply gain overnight. We are often overwhelmed with stories of people who have become famous for little to no observable reason, and this often leads many people to believe that success happens overnight. Nothing that grows overnight can be fully trusted in the daylight. It is in the process of weathering the storms, fighting the battles, and resisting the inevitable forces of doom that we qualify for the higher life. It is also on this journey that we are going to discover some things about ourselves and about God as He is continually developing us to manage the greater life.

Here is where it gets sticky. God does not tell you necessarily *how* He will do it. He only tells you that He *will* do it. God specializes in sharing what we need to know to keep us from messing up what we do not know. God reveals and conceals according to His created cosmic purpose. God is the lifeguard who ensures us that we will be safe even in the midst of chaos. God keeps, provides, and directs our journey in ways that baffle, confuse, and even sometimes hurt us.

This process is a journey of ups and downs. Instead of trying to control the journey, surrender to God's power and let surrender sustain you during the confusion. Grit, hard work, and prayer will be ready tools on your journey, but please understand that surrender is also needed and is often acquired on the way to destiny. God takes you on a journey of discovery and development that leads you to a higher life, but you must surrender in order to fully participate.

God has an interesting way of making His directions to you seem vague and incomplete. There is a good reason God does not feel the need to give you a detailed navigational system: He is offering to *be* your navigational system. God, the Creator of the universe, the definer of the ends of the Earth, and the topographer of your life's mountains, is offering to lead you on a journey into a future that is already designed. God is the navigational voice that directs you and I on when to turn and when to merge. God's navigation is specifically tuned to give each one of us a unique route to get us to where He desires us to be. Often, that direction is nebulous and nonsensical, but God still guides!

In Genesis 12:1, God gave Abram a very vague instruction: "Go to the land I will show you." Then God abruptly stopped talking about the directions and started promising Abram what following these directions would provide for him.

In the New Testament, when Peter decided he wanted to do greater by doing something that he had never done before — walking on water — Peter got a vague, one-word direction: "Come."

If you are going to walk this walk to become greater, sometimes you will have to learn how to walk on a word. Here is the promise God makes to you: He will do the showing if you will do the going. Many of us need a parade, a handcrafted invitation, and a guaranteed contract before we can act on God's Word. Sometimes a word is all you have! Maybe the only word you need to hear is "Go!" and that will set you free. We have to learn how to trust God enough to move, even on a word. We have to learn to abandon concrete mediocrity for the abundant uncertainty of the higher life. There are many things in life that only occur when we move toward them. Our faith is demonstrated in our response to vague instructions.

I was entering a convenience store to purchase a beverage, but as I approached the doors, there was no handle for me to grab. I saw an employee standing outside and asked him if the store was still open. He replied, "Keep walking." I felt as though he had blown off my question with such a short, vague answer. I was expecting something a little more clear and detailed. However, his simple words worked, and as I walked toward the doors, they opened automatically with a sensor. The door had not opened before because I had not walked close enough. His simple words, "Keep walking," had helped open the doors to where I was going. I hope that we do not miss the opening of the doors to our destinies because we refuse to listen to God's vague instructions.

When Jesus says, "Give us this day our daily bread," He clearly recognizes that God provides what we need when we need it, to sustain us for the day's journey. Likewise, when you wake up tomorrow, God will show you where to go. The day after that, and the next day, and the next day, God will show you what you need on those days. God will tell you how to pay your bills, will direct your path to work, and will provide you with enough gas to get to and from work. God is the God of forever and a day and the God of the day to day. God already has your provisions stored up and dispenses it to you as He sees fit. We need not worry about *whether* God will provide, but we do need to consider *how* we will manage it once He provides. God gives vague instructions like He gives the fowl nourishment for their journey: day by day, one morsel at a time, just as he leads us with one hazy and smoky revelation after another.

Furthermore, when God is talking to you, one word should be more than enough. Maybe the one word God is giving you about your marriage, your job, your business, or the ministry you are involved in is 'stay'. It's not a word we like to hear often, especially when we are desirous of change. 'Stay' is painful and frustrating when we desire and pray to roam free of the confines of laborious, dreary situations. Sometimes God's vague directions still manage to speak a word of 'stay' to a restless spirit. God is the initiator of new seasons and transitions, yet sometimes these goals can only be achieved when you decide to stay put and work things through, thereby fighting to stay together instead of fighting to leave.

Maybe the only word God is giving you about your future is 'trust'. Lack of trust is a cancerous feeling that erodes relationships and isolates people from authentic connection. Stephen Covey's book, *The Speed of Trust,* describes the power of trust and the peril of a lack thereof. Trust, in Covey's view, speeds things up, improves productivity, and is at the core of relationships. Trust is important, because when it is mutual among partners, deals can be done cheaper and faster, as a relationship of integrity and longevity lessens the need for strenuous checking and verification. The quality of the relationship and knowledge of the partner will create trust and confidence.

God's simple and vague word may be, "Trust Me." When we reflect on how faithful and timely God has been, trust should come easier. The more we trust God, the faster we are able to act on what God says and the quicker we are eligible to access the abundant life. If we do not trust God when He speaks five words, there is no guarantee we will listen to God's voice in any other format. Trust God when the night stalks and the stars hide. Trust God sitting in that courtroom. Trust God as you face problems your money cannot fix. Trust God on a word!

If you want a greater life, it will require the activation of your faith to trust in a God who does not elaborate in excessive detail. The level of faith we show cannot be based on what we know. It is not faith if we know all the details. Additionally, God is not always forthcoming with the plans, but that does not mean that God is 'free-styling' our existence. God knows the number of hairs on our head and all the mistakes you make and then pretends they never happened. God arranges for the daily meeting between the bird and the worm and for those hidden desires we suppress. God is actively leading us into the depths of His Will, but we are led, like Hansel and Gretel, with breadcrumbs of our partial understanding. God is holding the puzzle box and giving us one puzzle piece at a time.

God may not disclose all the details, but He does have a plan for every situation you will occupy. God doesn't make things up as He goes along. He knows the end from the beginning. He had Abraham's destination mapped out before he ever took the first step. He had His right arm outstretched to yank Peter up before he ever went underwater. Just because God does not show you the details does not mean He is without the details of our lives. Matthew 6:28 tells us that God provides constant clothing and nourishment for the lilies of the field. That being the case, then how much more will He do for you and I? You've got to approach this thing with faith, knowing that God has worked it all out in advance! Our job is to do what we need to do so that nothing hinders us from following the directions given to us for the journey.

It's about surrender. Surrender greets us when we continue to look at the life of the prophet Elisha in 1 Kings 19 and the chapters to follow. In the previous chapter, the prophet Elijah found Elisha, as God told him to. The trusted and faithful prophet of Yahweh looked back over his life's work and saw the mantle bearer of the prophetic leadership of God's people. He threw his prophetic coat around Elisha as a symbol of things to come. The mantle was a sign of a new season, increased responsibility, and retraining. The mantle was not just a garment draped upon the shoulders of men in the Middle Eastern world; it was a sign of the greatness passing from one prophet to another and from one generation to another.

God often affirms our calling through our connection to other people. The mantle was a point or object of connection. Elisha was working, attending to his daily tasks as a small business owner — which he was successful at, considering he had oxen, a crew of men, and a prophet. In fact, when the prophet threw a mantle upon him, Elisha was working, not looking for a mantle to be thrown on him. He was successful and happy in his current life. He had stability and peace of mind. He did not have to wander for miles, preach to the imperial powers of the Palestinian world, or do miracles. He was a man of routine. I think that it is safe to say that Elisha was living a good life. It is interesting to see that he was not looking for an encounter with the higher life, but the encounter came to him. In the middle of his toil, what he was *not* looking for found *him.*

When we keep our hands working in the areas of life that we know we have been assigned to, we unknowingly place ourselves in a position to connect with great people. It is easy to assume that those who run around seeking approval succeed in this world, but I have found that people who work hard often place themselves in positions to succeed far better than people who try to skip the hard work.

Elisha was not in the Elijah fan club, nor did he try to date Elijah's daughter to be one of the family. Elisha stuck to his work and stayed in his lane, and God gave him what he could not have gotten by any other means.

Elisha was working, and Elijah approached him and placed this mantle upon him. The mantle represented a choice. He was not asked if he wanted the mantle. He was not brought in for a consultation about the mantle. He was noticed and it was placed upon him. How do you handle the invitation to the higher life? Elisha chose to go with the prophet and to follow God. The Bible declares that Elisha left the oxen pulling his plow and was also prepared to leave his parents.

Notice that Elisha immediately walked away from his oxen and had only one request: to kiss his parents goodbye. He had made the choice to follow the direction God was assigning for his life. In order to make life greater, you have to be willing to take up the challenge of change. You have to be willing to trust what you do not know and what you have not seen. Change is the transportation to your new season, even if it makes you uncomfortable.

You have to be willing to experience the joy of being uncomfortable! Imagine the routine, consistent life Elisha had, yet he had no clue what he would be facing in the immediate future. Everything was about to change. His daily routine was about to be altered. The normal structure of his days was about to change. He was about to instantly change professions. He was leaving everything he had ever known, and it all happened in a moment, in an encounter.

It is not a stretch to say that Elisha's life changed in the twinkling of an eye.

As mature believers, we may realize that we are not joyful just because we love the things that happen for us. More important than superficial, carnal comfort, we must be uncomfortable — spiritually contented with the present but restless for God's future unfolding — to be joyful, because it reveals that God is growing, stretching, and using us. I am joyful because God allows me to grow. The reason that you are alive and are able to read this book is because God is not done with you yet!

Many people pray long prayers, rub lucky rabbit's feet, and play the same numbers in lottery every week to have their life change in such a fashion as Elisha's. The prophet of the land is telling him he is the next major prophet. He is being invited from life's audience onto history's stage to play a starring role. It is like keeping a racing car in your garage for years without touching it and then being asked to enter the Daytona 500 in it — *right now.* It is analogous to asking the player at the end of the bench, who has not ever played, to become your team's leading scorer — *right now!*

Elisha's world had changed. The deck of cards was being reshuffled. He only had time to say goodbye to his mother and father. His circle of influence and relationships was changing, as well. I realize that some people never get beyond their mediocrity because they do not like change. They resist it. They struggle against it. They retreat into bunkers of nostalgia, wishing for the good old days. They are not water resistant;

they are change resistant. Those people who never leave the past behind forfeit their future.

It happens with marriages. People refuse to change because they make excuses about why they *will* not (not *cannot)* change their behavior. "I was this way when you met me." or, "My mother was this way and I cannot help it." These are responses from a person who refuses to change.

It happens in businesses, which must adapt with the times. Many great businesses fail because they refuse to change. Not forecasting where their field was headed leads many businesses to close because of a lack of change. I can remember very vividly when Blockbuster Videos came into existence. There was one right around the corner from my parents' home. I would run there at least three times a week to rent videos. The lines would be crazy long, as people were excited about this newfound idea of renting movies. Now, some twenty plus years later, Blockbuster has gone out of business and all of their stores have closed. When an executive of Blockbuster was asked what happened, his reply proves my assertion. He said that they had gone out of business because they had refused to change to keep up with the times. When you refuse to change, you are foreclosing on your own future.

It happens in churches. Many mainline denominations all over the country are closing their doors because they've refused for years to engage the times. While many aren't closing their doors, you can lay down on a pew any given Sunday during worship, because there has been a mass exodus from that church which remains traditional. My Bishop,

Bishop Paul S. Morton, Sr. says that all tradition amounts to is "frozen success" that we thaw out to try to prove we have something going on.

Being resistant to change is much like having shackles around one's legs. They keep our world small because we are unable to go anywhere, but after a while, we make use of the world we have and begin to embrace the chains as a reality that will not change, instead of seeking to change the situation. We like to stick with what we have always done and what we already know. It is sad but true.

I am not advocating for a full-scale rejection of the past. That is unwise and detrimental to your growth. I believe we should honor what we have always done by standing on the shoulders of it and building upon it, but not by staying in it. Many of us, under the guise of memory, bury ourselves in 'yesterday' because we are hiding from 'tomorrow'. If we consistently talk about past methods and memories without a sense of distance from them, we will never live in the present and will relegate our future to unattainable realities.

I challenge you to not build memories so tall that you are unable walk away from them, nor should you worship only what you respect or understand. As you move forward, let that past situation go! Learn the lessons! Cry the tears! But, please . . . move on! Let God change you by allowing change to come through you.

It is also hard to embrace change because we make excuses. Humans are prone to making excuses. The biggest enemy to greatness is 'the excuse'. What is the excuse? It becomes the crutch you use to remain comfortable where you are. Excuses allow responsible people to avoid responsibility. Excuses rob people of the power to change. Excuses erode the confidence of your colleagues and friends. Excuses are cavities in the seemingly beautiful teeth of destiny. The 'excuse', without mask or gun, has robbed people of their dreams, goals, and their access to God's best.

If I asked you to name the most common excuses you have heard, you might say, "We've never done it that way before." Another classic excuse is, "I do not think that will work because I did not think of it." Excuses are instant answers for people who have no desire to imagine new possibilities. It is easy to find fault with others and critique their excuses, but before we seek to exhume the speck from our friend's eye, we need to attend to the log of excuses that hinders our vision and blocks our ability to take responsibility for our own lives.

When Elisha requests time to go home and kiss his parents good-bye, Elijah doesn't tell him *not* to. He simply says, "When you go back, remember what I have done for you." He wants Elisha to reflect upon the amazing opportunity that this mantle signifies, that he is next in a line of prophetic succession, a larger occurrence than he can ever imagine.

Elijah knew that Elisha's going home to his parents would be a risk, because Elisha's parents would feel protective about their son's unknown future they do not understand and that does not involve them. They were not involved in the encounter between Elijah and Elisha and do not know the situation, but their sincere and well-meaning ignorance could steer Elisha away from what he has been ordained to do.

So Elijah says to Elisha, "Do what you have to do, but just in case they try to talk you out of it, remember the significance of what I have done for you and what it means for your future."

When it comes time to make critical decisions about sacrifice and commitment, be careful of the good and bad company you keep. Both may love you, but bad company can cause you to miss your God moment. They love you to death in the literal and metaphorical sense. People who you love and who love you will seek to give you the best advice possible, but if they did not hear what God told you, they can, in love, talk you out of what God said. These same people can love and smother you until it is hard to breathe a fresh breath.

Now, do not get me wrong; advice is good. It is always good to seek out wisdom. The Bible encourages gaining wisdom in concert with others. But at the end of the day, when God has spoken, I have learned that I do not need advice on what to do. I may need your prayers to help me do it, but not your advice about *if* I should do it. I may need your advice on strategizing it but not your advice on doing it.

People will love you away from your destiny if you let them, because they don't understand what you are about to do. You may be trying to start a business, but people keep telling you that this is an unfavorable time to start a business. If God has instructed you to do it now, then do it now! There is never a perfect time to start a business. Waiting on the perfect time will make you miss out on God's time, every time! There is never a perfect time for anything, but there will be a God ordained time.

Many people, in their need for control, wait for the perfect time, when in fact, the perfect time is 'when God says'. We feel that we know better than God about when to act. God is not consulting us on our desired preference of journey or timing of the journey. It may not be the time you wanted to go back to school, but if God says "Go" — you go!

Elisha was confronted with the opportunity to have his life changed. The mantle by the prophet was placed upon him. Then he did something strange in 1 Kings 19:21. The Bible says that he killed his oxen as a sacrifice, *and* he burned his plowing equipment. He owned these oxen and the equipment. Faced with the choice of following God or continuing on a path of amazing mediocrity (good enough), Elisha chose to follow Elijah. To confirm and cement his commitment, he destroyed the symbols of his old life.

There is a major life principle in what Elisha did that we all need to hear when it comes to walking away from being good enough. Elisha refused to keep his future open to interference from his past. He made a decisive break from his old life and everything that represented stability and the predictability of his old life. He sacrificed his plow to the fire, totally incinerating it to ensure that he would not be able to return to the life he once knew. He surrendered his plan for his life as his plow burned.

If you want to have the greater life, you have to learn how to burn your plow. Your plow is what chains you to the ordinary, to your past, to the suitable and the comfortable. Your plow is what keeps you in your present when your present needs to be your past.

I did not say bury, hide, or dismantle your plow. I did not say that you should put your plow in a locker, storage, or under the bed. In order to become our best, we must destroy and delete the plows of our lives. Maybe the plow is a person; delete their number! Maybe the plow is a job; work where God has called you to work! Maybe the plow is a habit; kick the habit and stop letting the habit kick you! Maybe the plow is a ministry in the church; get where your gift fits.

Why is it important to surrender the plow? You have to get tired of the plow and realize that what God is offering is better than what you wanted for yourself! Do not live an average life. Do not do average things. God is calling us to the higher life, flying twenty-thousand feet above mediocrity.

There is a great song we used to sing when I was a child and when hymns seemed to still be desirable (Yes, that was sarcasm.). It said, "I have decided to follow Jesus; no turning back, no turning back". Following Jesus means that you can't turn back, and to make sure you don't turn back, you have to burn the plows of your present good life in order to go to the higher life the Lord is calling you to.

Let's explore some examples of plows:

Your present job, if it isn't in line with what God has called you to do, is a plow. Often, for the sake of security, the pressures of debt, or the need for the affirmations of others, we work in jobs that suck the soul from us and antagonize our desires for freedom. We work jobs for a check, but what is the point of a nice paycheck if we spend half of it on alcohol that we drink to tolerate the job? You would save money and feel better by doing what God has gifted you to do. You may make less, but your happiness will improve and your liver will thank you.

Another plow is a hidden but dangerous one: a life that is too safe. Many people have not become all that God intends because they play life too close to the chest. Their refusal to have faith and trust God beyond their senses keeps them tied to the past. Life was safe; their family's demands were manageable; their pay periods always corresponded to the bills; they saved and invested, but now God is calling them to move, relocate, or redraw circles of friendship. Playing it safe ensures a shortened horizon and a condensed outlook for the future. As they say at Spades tables all over the land, "Scared money don't make no money."

You cannot step into your new life until you first destroy connections to whatever is keeping you bound to systems of mediocrity and relationships of compromise. We must be bold in our response to the plows of our life. They have been faithful to us and essential in how we have arrived here, but, because of their past utility, they are dangerous threats to our future because they provide mental and physical connections to life on a lower level. The plow could have triggered Elisha to go back, therefore he would rather risk it all on God than hedge his bets with his past. He would rather trust God fully and see how it ends than not trust God enough to leave the past behind.

The real risk is not in launching into a new life or in following God's leading. The largest risk is staying in your old life, full of the 'ordinary' and stagnation. While you have your share of anxiety, busily counting the cost of burning the plow, you should be counting the cost of *not* burning the plow. You will miss out on even more if you stay like you are right now.

Just in case you start to have second thoughts about what it will take to be greater, let me tell you what is at risk if you do not:

Greater confidence in God. Often, not surrendering our plows keeps us bound to the past and reaffirms an artificial confidence in ourselves. When we do not burn our plows and surrender our plans to God, we tend to worship the past and exhibit more confidence in what we have done instead of what God will do. We need to separate from and surrender our past, which forces us to trust in what is to come and not what already was. God is seeking to get to know us more, but we have to be willing to separate from our past. We need to have more confidence in God, but often our plows of the past rob us of the chance to know God in a deeper way.

Greater authority in God. The child of God must be mindful of the power and authority that comes from our relationship with God. Being children of God gives us authority to take control over our situations and ourselves. Too many people walk around in weak and defeated postures because they do not walk with a sense of authority and purpose. There is power and strength in knowing that God has given you the vision, provision, and clarity of mind to make a good decision.

Greater clarity of your calling. Many people know, whether they admit it or not, what their life's calling is. However, they do not have a clue as to why they are here on Earth. By not risking everything and trusting God, those questions of calling will always linger, because we will not be closely connected enough to God to see what we are designed to do. Relationships reveal the heart. The closer people are, the more they share and the less words often need to be spoken. By not having faith in God, we are not able to engage God in ways that will allow us the closeness to God to see our purpose. Playing it safe has not shown you what your life is supposed to do, so it may be time to trust God fully and get some clarity on what your calling is and how to execute it!

Greater influence over people around you. Why should someone follow you? Why should people listen to you? What validates your voice in a crowd? People who play it safe and lean on their own understanding can be great leaders and influence people, but to what ends? Where are you leading people? If you have people looking to *you*, whom do *you* look to? Trusting God creates a calm and peace that draws people to you. When you truly step out on God's Word and live the abundant life, you will not have to shout to be heard; your opinion will be sought. You will not have to listen to rumors and after-meeting commentary; you will have the substance of character to be invited into the conversation at the big meeting. Trusting God in your personal life radiates through you; people will seek you out and enjoy your company. Do not risk *not* maximizing your godly influence over people because you do not seek to trust God for yourself.

Greater joy in knowing that you're in the time of God's blessing. I have a sports metaphor that I think illustrates this.

I am an avid football fan. Football plays have always intrigued me. They have all types of strange words and numbers, and everything they say means something. When many teams call a 'pass play', the quarterback tries to throw the ball to the wide receiver who is open. He is throwing to the direct location of the wide receiver. Other types of 'pass plays' are called 'timing routes'. Timing routes are passes that are thrown not to the wide receiver's body but to a particular place on the field. Even if the defensive back tightly covers the wide receiver, the quarterback trusts the wide receiver to get to the spot and beat the coverage. The pass is thrown with the confidence that the receiver's timing will match the quarterback's. If they are not on the same page, it will be an interception; when thrown properly, it is a big play. The key to a timing route is the receiver's ability to "create space" between himself and the defender.

When we trust God fully, rely on divine timing, and follow the strange plays God designs, success is often imminent. God is throwing the ball to you, but will you be able to make the play? What plows do you need to "create space" from in order to be at the right place to catch the blessing God is throwing? When will you be able to trust God to give you what you need when you need it? If you give up because you lose faith in God, the defensive backs of opposition will take your blessing and score a touchdown for the other team. God has designed

WHEN GOOD ISN'T GOOD ENOUGH

these plays for your success. Surrender your will and what you believe things look like, and rest in the knowledge that you are in God's timing. If you faint not, God will bless you.

Surrender your plow to the fire. Surrender your will to God. Surrender those love letters to the shredder. Surrender that child to the able arms of God. Surrender your marriage to counseling. Burn the remnants of mediocrity, compromise, and apathy. Walk away from the sweet seduction of average.

It is interesting that when people surrender, they throw up their hands. It is a demonstration of a lack of control and ability to act. When little children desire to be picked up by someone, they raise their arms in a similar fashion. Maybe that child has more sense than we do. That child realizes that they cannot get where they need to get on their own power, in their current condition. So what do they do? They raise their arms in an appeal to someone higher and stronger than themselves, asking that person to lift them up.

The only way I will get where I need to be is to leave the realm of my ability, surrender, raise my arms, and ask for help that is bigger and stronger than me. Surrender, raise your hands, and allow your Heavenly Father to meet you at the place of surrender.

SWEAT THE SMALL STUFF

Elisha made the decision to follow his divine destiny into something greater. This journey into a seemingly unscripted life of abundant living was a series of choices.

It is not enough to make one choice in the direction of God's best; the victory is earned in the successive steps we give to God and all the times we tell Him 'yes'. Elisha had a good, stable job, but to stay at that job when 'greater' was waiting for him made stability the enemy. Stability, and the comfort that stability brings, is the perfect mix of temptation for most people.

We live in a world where life is about consuming things that are designed for our comfort. Comfort is a driving motivation for our daily labor. We want the new car with the seat warmer to quickly warm us when the weather is ferociously bitter. Few people desire to live lives of discomfort and complete denial of the enjoyments of life. The problem arises when, because we over-value our pleasure and fear of the unknown, we allow stability to cripple our ability to conceive of anything beyond our sense of comfort. Many of us worship comfort and hide from the responsibilities of the greater life because we would have to go beyond our comfort zone.

Some of us need stability because we have lived lives of instability. Maybe you have struggled all your life. You have been working, saving, planning, and denying yourself the small joys of life. You are tired of moving from apartment to apartment, escaping eviction at every turn. You have decided to clean up your credit and save money to buy a house. God is telling you to not buy the house because he has more for you. You buy the house, a symbol of stability, and instead of chasing after God, your need for security and stability will be all you have left. I know life seems shaky and the waves of life make you unsure and unsettled about leaving stability, but when you settle, all you have is all you will ever have. You should want more because you know more is out there, and God wants to make sure you are ready for it.

The song of stability did not seduce Elisha. He burned his plow and his connection to his previous life, to ensure that during times of temptation to quit the journey to greater, he would have nothing of his past to fall back on.

I have noticed that many people, once they free themselves from the plow of their past, find themselves stuck in the next phase of their lives. In my estimation, there are two reasons why well-intentioned people get stuck after they burn their plows: They do not think big enough, and they do not start small enough.

Too many well-meaning people do not dream big enough. Their dreams are relegated to the cozy but claustrophobic world they currently occupy. They cannot think of owning the business they work for. They refuse to see the good in life. They are able to quickly count the reasons 'why not' instead of finding reasons 'why'. Dreaming small dreams defeats the very purpose of a dream.

We, as a collective body of humanity, must dream larger than being rich and bathing in the excesses of material consumption. We have to dream of a world that is not more philanthropic but more just. We need to dream of a world in which we are better stewards of natural resources, instead of wasting the fruits of an ever-living Earth. We have to avoid the trap of dreaming about the small and petty things of the world and dream more expansive dreams that better not only our immediate context, but also the world as a community.

Dreaming big is a major component of the abundant life, because, without imagination, how can we understand abundance? The tag team partner to dreaming big is the seemingly oxymoronic step of starting small. I know this is unpopular, but it is nonetheless true. We often dream large dreams but avoid the small and laborious steps and details that form the foundation of the great dream. The world is not in need of people who dream large dreams. Dreaming is free, sweatless, and pleasurable. There is no shortage of people who have ideas to make great sums of money. There are many people with novel ideas to remedy the world's critical issues. We won't see God's bigger vision fulfilled in our lives simply because we spend more time thinking bigger thoughts. We don't attain greater things simply by lying on the couch and concentrating on the possibilities of a better life or set aside a specific time to pray about it. Don't get me wrong; you have to be willing to think big, but the active ingredient of God's greater work in us and through us is our willingness to start *small*.

You have to be willing to believe that God is big enough to call you to something greater than where you are right now, or to do greater at what you are already doing. Even when that 'something greater' has been nowhere in your expectations or radar, God can cause 'greater' in every area of your life.

There is a principle that will help you understand your current season: The small start principle. Big dreams without a small, solid start are nothing but daydreams. God initiates the biggest changes in our lives through the smallest parts.

It is a principle that manifests in the Earth. Everything big started little. An oak tree began as an acorn. A six-foot man began as a tiny embryo in his mother's womb. A baby elephant is still large, but small compared to what it shall be. You have to be willing to start small! Too many people want to start big; they sit around waiting for their big break. There is no microwave blessing or Hot Pocket miracle for this. Small steps and humble beginnings contain the fundamental building blocks of the abundant life. The honesty that you learn when you are between funds makes you credible when your finances straighten out. The discipline you showed as a student, studying under the dim light of the library, will be displayed when you are able to intelligently articulate your educated opinion. Just because you did not start out on the mountaintop does not mean that you will not get there.

Everything you possess is a starting point. Start with whatever you have. Stop wishing and hoping to be someplace else. The faster we wake up and make the best use of where we are, the faster we can get to where God designed for us to be. Do not be like the man in Jesus' parable who had one talent and refused to use it. When you use whatever you have been given, more will come! If we do not use what we have, how can we expect more?

Jesus' life began in a stable, but he did not stay there. David only had a slingshot, but he became the king of Israel. Joseph, son of Jacob, was sold as a slave, but he became the Prime Minister of Egypt. The widow of Zarephath had only a small pancake, but she sowed it into the work of God and created a continuous supply during famine. Whatever you have been given is enough to create anything you have been promised when you use what you have been given properly and obediently.

Zechariah 4:10 warns us not to despise small beginnings. Often, we despise small things and unceremonious beginnings because we allow other people's estimation of our lives to become our own estimation of what God has called us to do. People may look down on your mode of transportation. You may be reading this on public transportation, but do not allow anyone to make you feel bad about your small beginnings. You are still in school when your friends have already graduated and landed good jobs and your parents do not agree with your major. Do what God said and make the most of the season of small beginnings. Do not allow other people's baggage to become your baggage. How they feel about your small beginnings is none of your business, anyway! You have to make the most of what you have! Whatever you possess today is enough to create anything else you will ever want in your future. You must know how to use it and be obedient with it, but do not despise it.

All of this growth cannot happen without faith. You have got to have faith enough to believe that whatever God tells you to do with whatever you have will be enough to get you to the greater life. Most people who are in business started small and as their own only employee; most married couples didn't start off in a big house; many CEOs worked in lower or middle management for years before having the skills to earn the top spot. You didn't start off earning a Master's degree. You had to put in work and have faith that God would supply in response to your faithful obedience.

It is important that we define what faith is and what faith is not. Faith isn't a state of mind. It's a course of action rooted in obedience. Faith is work. Faith is not wishing and hoping. Faith is not requesting a miracle dishtowel from a television prophet. Faith is not sneaking off to see a psychic to discern the mind of God. Faith is the evidence of what you expect. Faith is about working toward what God has shown. We can say that we have faith in God, but if we are not acting — because faith is a verb — then we are not living a life of faith. You can see faith. Faith is tangible and observable.

If you have faith that God will help you buy a house, I should see evidence in your credit score. If you have faith God will bring you a spouse, you have to become the right person, whether the right person comes for you or not. Faith is seen in how we live. Our lived faith is on display and tells the world if we are merely wishing on a star or believing in the Son. Can people see your faith?

The next lesson I see in the life of the prophet Elisha as he chose to live the greater life was his ability to trust God for bigger things than anyone around him dared to believe. He looked at every obstacle as an opportunity to prove that God is greater than the confines of the situation. That is one of the principles your faith has to hinge upon if you are going to commit to the greater life. Elisha looked beyond what was visible and began to step out on that which was invisible.

We are responsible for the way we see the world and how we respond to what we see. Elisha did not allow what was missing all around him to define all that would be around him. My heart breaks when I see gifted people restricted because they cannot see past their immediate context. No one in their family went to college, and now they do not believe they are college material. No one in their family has ever had a happy marriage, and now they refuse to seriously date. It hurts to see how amazing and gifted people become mentally, emotionally, and physically constricted, often rendering them unable to see the sunlight peeking through the overcast sky.

There are many people, and the number increases everyday, who are born into difficult and depressing circumstances. As the world simultaneously grows warmer through environmental change and colder in how we treat one another, the climate is too harsh for survival. Abuse, drug use, broken homes, and distinct disadvantages are hallmarks of a changing world. I am writing to arouse your sense of self-worth. I want to speak to the part of you that refuses to live like the people you grew up with. There is a spark on the inside that makes you dream of visiting Paris at night or trying something new. Do not let the limitations around you keep you limited in how you see your future. Our God is bigger than whatever you see around you!

Elisha did not just believe in the principle of small things, *he did something about it.* The action-oriented approach of Elisha shows us that miracles are not magic tricks. Miracles are the divine results of small steps of faith-filled preparation. Small steps and hard work will always precipitate a move of God. Human action prepares the way for supernatural favor.

We often make the concept of experiencing a breakthrough sound spooky and mysterious. You can run around church and foam at the mouth. You can wear all white and speak in more tongues than a translator, but if you refuse to do the small, tedious, mundane, and ordinary things, there will be no breakthrough. We must do the small things! We have to take seriously the foundation we are setting. We cannot ask for a big blessing without the small steps to support it.

King Joram ruled over Israel in the time known as 'The Divided Monarchy', or 'Southern and Northern Israel'.

The once unified nation of Israel was divided, fulfilling the prophecy of the Lord. When the king of Moab rebelled against him, Joram enlisted King Jehoshaphat of Judah and the King of Edom. This had the makings of a huge war. But while preparing for combat, something happened that caused them to face not just a terrifying foe, but a terrifying fate. They ran out of water and were soon dying of thirst.

Running out of water is a major predicament. Water is the most valuable commodity for human thriving. If there is no water, there is no life. The men and soldiers fighting for their survival faced a shortage of the one thing without which they could not function. Water nourished their animals, refreshed the men, and supplied nutrients to the surrounding areas. They were facing the fight of their lives and found themselves lacking the fundamental resources they needed for survival.

The crisis drove Joram to look for help from God. Don't miss this. He was not looking for God as much as he was looking for a solution. Joram found himself in such a bind that he had no choice but to seek out God. God was the only force that could intervene in such a dire situation. Many of us know the feeling of our world falling apart and seeing that God is the only intervening force that can save us. Maybe that is how we met God, not because we were looking for a relationship, but because we needed resources. It is the frustration of our resources (material and relational) that often draws us closer to God. Joram was looking for help. He needed a miracle. He was in need, but instead of just gaining resources, he was going to be part of the miracle itself.

Jehoshaphat, a king partnering with Joram in this war effort, asked if there was a prophet who could consult with God for them. That was wise. Before engaging in a major situation, Jehoshaphat inquired of God about what to do.

Joram let him know about this new prophet on the scene by the name of Elisha, who had taken the place of Elijah. According to the biblical record, Elisha was God's prophet, the receiver of the prophetic mantle. They went to see Elisha, who was not overly sympathetic to their cause, but because he was loyal to Jehoshaphat, he chose to seek the Lord. He asked for a musician, because there is something about background music that provides peace for meditation. It facilitates sensitivity to the presence of God.

He began to tell them what God had told him. He confirmed that water would flow from Edom by the time the sun came up the next morning and that they and their animals would have something to drink. The drought was almost over!

I want to speak life into you, because the drought is almost over for you as well. I know you have been wondering when the seasons of dryness and frustration will end. The drought is almost over. Maybe you have been heartbroken to the very depths of your being. The drought is almost over. I understand that you are trying to hide tears of depression and shame because of where you are and how you hate where you may be. The drought is almost over.

The prophet in the text is telling people who are on the brink of defeat that what they need is on its way. In similar fashion, I believe that these words will awaken the slumbering dreams inside you and remind you that you have had water before and that you will have water again. The only reason why this is considered a drought is due to the fact that they have experienced water before. It may have been a long time since you felt refreshed and rejuvenated, but the drought is almost over!

Now watch the instructions from the Lord. This is where the text becomes truly interesting. Elisha prophesized that the drought would end, and in II Kings 3:16, he instructed them to prepare for the coming rain by filling the valley with ditches.

Dig ditches! Digging ditches seems small, but it is the key to every blessing that God has for us. Let me give you a few principles from that:

When God has promised you greater things, you do not wait for a sign to appear before you respond. The king wanted a miracle, and they would receive a miracle, but first they had to fulfill a work order. It was as if God said, "If you really believe I'm going to do what I told you I would, then get busy! Show me your faith and I will show you my faithfulness. If you dig the ditches, I will send the rain." Only God can send the rain, but we must dig the ditches. We must do the work. We must prepare ourselves to receive God's best.

We are always looking for signs to validate what God said when we *know* what God said. We wait for the phone to ring with the right call. We open the Bible, hoping that the page we turn to will speak to us. We are looking around for a sign to show us how to live and what to do next. God is raising our level of expectation and challenging our maturity when we only are given work to do and not a sign about why we are doing it.

Listen, God will tell us what to do, but He will obscure why we do it. God is saying that you need to finish your degree. You may not know why God is saying that, but you have been praying for more resources. You will not get paid more without the degree, so in order to answer your prayer, you have to prepare by doing what God said. You may not get a sign, but you have enough to work with. Do what you can!

In order to prepare, *we will see the power of a plan.* Notice that in the text, Elisha told the armies to dig ditches. Digging ditches shows the power of a plan. A plan is a written list of arranged actions necessary to achieve your desired goal. We must plan! Life cannot be an exercise in ad-libbing. We have to strategize, plan, and think through how we will handle what God gave us. If God sent the rain to the Israelites but they had not adequately prepared by having a plan, the blessing would flood them and curse them more than bless them. Further, the ditches that needed to be dug would allow them to hold onto the blessings beyond the moment in which they appeared. Not having a plan for God-given resources is an invitation for mismanagement and waste.

They needed a plan for ditches for water that was not yet coming. We cannot prepare without a plan. A sound plan is the response to God's promise. If we do not develop a plan, we have to wonder if we believe what God has shown us. Dig, baby, dig!

Stop getting mad with the banker because the bank will not loan you the money to start your business because you do not have a business plan. Your parenting will always be reactive to the problems of life because you do not have a plan for your children's development. Families need order and direction, but if the head of the house is without a plan, what is the rest of the household supposed to do?

It is safe to say that your money will not last without a plan. Maybe your life is in complete and utter disarray because you do not have a plan for it. *Our lives often reflect the time and energy we commit to planning it.* A messy life is often comprised of messy decisions guided by the moment instead of by a plan. Why should someone pledge his or her life to you if you have no idea where you are going or how you will get there? A goal without a plan is a wish. Where is your plan? Where is God leading you? How can you get there? What can you do to prepare?

Plan your work and work your plan! This response to God's promise ensures that we are partners with God in the promise. We are actively engaged in the success and fruition of God's desire. Planning our work demonstrates that we take God seriously, and working our plan means we take ourselves seriously. We need to engage in holistic responses to God's promises. Planning your work and working your plan is a holistic response. Value God's Word and value your own work.

The text goes on to tell us that God supplied rain to every place where they had dug a ditch. God was telling them, "I will send rain to every place that you prepare for it. Every place that you have planned for increase will be supplied." It is not about where you have shouted and where you have prayed. Though prayer is important, prayer alone does not change situations. The text clearly shows us that God provides miracles and increase to places that are prepared for it. God is not interested in our shout but our shovel. Our lip service and all-night praise sessions are beautiful and ornamental, but *God honors faith,* and it is seen in the shoveling — the preparation for God's promise — rather than in the shouting about the promise.

I would rather shovel for what I know is coming than just shout about it, because eventually I will tire of shouting and still have to dig. If I shovel and dig now, I can shout when I get what God has for me.

Where is your shovel? What do you need to prepare for? Do not wait. Dig right now. Do not let another aimless day wander past or a meandering night sneak away without getting your plan together and working it!

Having a plan may be the reason why you are where you are today. You may be the only person in your family to have graduated from college. You may have been the first to leave your neighborhood. You may be the only person of your ethnicity, gender, or age in your area at work. You have been able to persevere because you had a plan. Having a plan when disorder is the order kept you from giving up and letting go. Having a plan, especially God's plan for you, provides a sense of comfort, because no matter what you must face, you know where you are heading. God has watered your life in places where you have planned and prayed. To God be the glory for how God's plan has kept you sane and safe in a crazy world.

Beyond the power of planning, the last major principle that is considered a small thing is that decisions create events. *You have to learn to make decisions that create a desired future instead of a desired present.* Too many of us make decisions based on the present. Many people find themselves in future debt because of present decisions. We all know people, and maybe we should include ourselves, who have purchased things that we did not need nor could afford in the present in order to pay for it in the future. Many rich and famous people have squandered untold millions on fleeting pleasures. Not only the rich suffer from this, but many of us have spent ourselves, and subsequently our future, on the need to have things now. We consume now only to pay later.

Here is an interesting thought: Many people of goodwill and earnest intention choose to consume now, buy now, enjoy now, and offer their future as payment. Whenever we decide based on the immediacy of the moment, we are buying that present moment with our future. We are spending what we could be in the future on something that may have little or no value even in the present. If I purchase a car that I cannot afford, I am offering the next five years of my future income to the finance company for something I cannot even enjoy because I cannot afford it. I would have traded my future on a fleeting feeling that a new car provides, but that choice produced a long-term outcome I would not want.

Do not make decisions on a desired present! The present slips away quicker than lightning across the sky, and just that fast a choice of instant gratification alters the future. Many of us have spent so much energy living for the weekend that we forget that unless we die or Jesus comes back, we will have to face life after that moment. Stop living for the present. Live with a plan. Live with purpose. Live knowing that the choices you make create outcomes you will have to face.

I have heard it said that when we make bad choices, we lose control of the consequences. Poor choices are the bricks that have built the places where we currently live. Maybe you are where you are because of the constant stacking of bad choices. You went to prison. You got a divorce. You engaged in behavior that has changed your life. You can start to make good choices that produce life and not death. Choosing life is about deciding that bad choices will only make things worse. It is harder to change tomorrow than today.

I am changing and making different choices. I am making adjustments in my preaching style to help prolong my health. Recently, a colleague remarked about how I utilize PowerPoint slides in my sermon. I am not as animated and demonstrative as I used to be, and I have altered my pace some. Little did he know that I was not preaching to aesthetically wow people in the present and die tomorrow. I am not interested in trying to do what will not benefit me for the long run. I am not preaching for today; I am preaching with my eyes on tomorrow, and I want to get there intact.

The older I get, the more I change. I am sure it should be that way. I have to make adjustments that are for my future success. The older we become, the more we should be mindful of the future. The days are drawing near the end for some, but what I have learned from those older than myself is an unshakable respect for their ability to change. The previous generations have been called Colored, Negro, Afro-American, Blacks, and African-Americans. The individuals in their eighties and nineties have seen both Jim Crow and the first African-American president. Many of them went from no phone to a landline phone to a cell phone. These dedicated men and women's abilities to change with the times and plan for the future has placed all of us on solid ground. We must pass that same good fortune along to our children.

Don't forget this. Everything you are presently doing will benefit your present or your future. The choice is yours. You need to resolve to make decisions that will benefit your future. That's what digging a ditch was about: The future.

Much like computer software that must be updated and hardware that may need replacement, our thinking must also be updated and even replaced. We must reprogram our thinking to distance. We have to elongate our perspectives. We have to think about our daily decisions with our eyes on the horizon. How will this choice appear when I examine it through the perspective of distance? Distance brings perspective to the immediacy of the moment. Using words like 'next year', or 'in a year', and 'tomorrow' helps us to properly judge our situation.

That may seem hard for many to embrace, but I also know that all of us desire something greater until we have to start digging for it. Prepare for the move of God before God makes the first move. People run from conference to conference and revival to revival, sowing financial seeds and being so much under the influence of the Holy Spirit that they float around, *but* when they are asked to do the work, live the life, and exhibit the character of what they are praying for *before it comes,* it is not as fun anymore.

Preachers cannot stand before God's people and not study. You cannot be Husband of the Year and Father of the Decade if you do not come home at night, or if your family does not trust you. We want greater business opportunities but offer subpar service. We want greater friendships but we entertain people who always tear us down. We want the promotion but will not put forth our best effort on a presentation that will give us the promotion. We say we want greater, but are we doing greater hard work? What small steps are we working on to secure the greater life?

Lastly, we cannot expect God to entrust us with a big dream if we cannot be trusted with a small start. What are you working on? What ditches are you digging right now? Scripture tells us that the abundance we receive will be in proportion to the preparation we make. Wars in the ancient Middle East went on for years. They needed water to last the duration of their situation. That meant they had to dig with all their might as deep as they could, because every place, every inch of ground they prepared, would be full of God's blessing.

The digging of the ditches seems so small and minute. For others, digging ditches of preparation seems foolish and nonsensical. Regardless of the various perspectives, too many people despise small things and difficult beginnings.

God is a big God, and I see the abundance of rain in your life! Start digging and experience the outpouring of God's best for you! Maybe God is calling you to dig in the area of your self-confidence or your worldview. For some, the controlling nature of their personality has alienated friends and family. Embrace the work. God is calling you to a life that is worth the hard work. Your labor will not be in vain. The foolishness you feel as you dig will fade away as you see that every ditch you have dug is full of water.

Dig with tears in your eyes!

Dig when your muscles hurt!

Dig with people laughing at you!

Dig when you have to ask your mother to watch your kids while you go to school!

Dig when you finally engage professional counseling to deal with your mental health!

Dig when you eat what you *have* to instead of what you *want* to!

Dig when digging seems small, because God is glorified in the small things!

THE EXCEPTION MAKES EXCEPTIONAL

W henever you read stories of great business leaders, owners, or franchise-starters whose businesses now have national acclaim, you will quickly discover that many of them never became superstar names, but their businesses are part of the American landscape. If I asked who Dave Thomas is, many would have only a faint idea. If I asked about your knowledge of Wendy's, the fast food restaurant, the likelihood of recollection would be much higher. Many of us have eaten flame-broiled patties from Burger King but are unfamiliar with its founder.

This makes sense when we notice that the life beyond 'just good enough' for so many of us is unfortunately and erroneously characterized in terms of fame, fortune, substance, and accouterments. Too many of us want to be known and famous, never realizing that if we live the greater life, what we have been given to do by God will take us further than we could ever imagine.

Tyler Perry, the acclaimed African-American entertainer, entrepreneur, and media mogul, spent many years self-producing his plays with little traction or crowd support. He sacrificed and worked hard to grow his business, even if he had to do without. We judge the greater life on the scoreboard of superficiality, assuming that the 'stuff' is the goal. If that model were true, Tyler Perry would have been considered a failure. Now he is a multi-millionaire, shaping our culture, because he understands that the person with the most 'stuff' and the kid with the most toys does not win. Though he has those things and is experiencing life beyond 'good enough', he would attest to the fact that 'stuff' is not the greater life. The newspapers are full of stories of extremely wealthy people struggling with life's meaning, even though they have everything. You can have all of those things and not be living the greater life.

When it comes to the greater life in Christ, it begins with what you *say* to God and results in what you *do* for God. I know that sounds strange. Listen, God is concerned with our response to our purpose; will it be 'yes' or 'no'?

You can say, "Yes, God, I will follow You wholeheartedly into the greater things that You are calling me into, no matter what it looks like." This is the biggest and scariest thing a person can imagine saying. It is like signing up for a lifetime journey of trusting in the dark and walking where this is no path. Surrendering to God by saying 'yes' opens the windows of the soul, allowing fresh air to circulate. Many of us need to surrender to God and offer a 'yes', because our soul needs to breathe. Saying 'yes' to God is not about stumbling into a dark curtain of confusion; it is about allowing the life and light of God to show you a way of higher living that you were created to inhabit.

We can say, "No, God, I don't want to burn my plows, dig my ditches, and follow You to a place where I have to live my life by faith and not by sight." It is a basic choice that has long-lasting ramifications. Declining the opportunity to partner with God in the higher life hurts us. I believe that many of the people who tell God 'no' are afraid of being disoriented by change. I have to admit, being a pastor, it seems as if more often than not, the word 'change' is the biggest enemy in the church.

Change is a disorienting experience, because we can lose the landmarks of our lives. The places and habits that have been constant and sure are no longer available. We are unable to see our lives apart from who we used to be and how life was configured. Because it will require some change, our natural instinct to embracing better is not always a 'yes'. Do not miss out on 'greater' because you are afraid to leave 'lesser', just because of the changes it will bring to your life!

Saying 'no' to God speaks to how much faith we have in God.

What moving beyond 'good enough' requires of you will depend on your life and what God is calling you to do. You cannot measure the actions and sacrifices of someone else and determine whether or not they are on to something greater or lesser than you. Maybe you were always compared to the 'favorite' sibling and now you never feel fulfilled with the accomplishments of your journey. Instead of being thankful for the many blessing you have, you are in a constant inner competition with someone who is unaware of your deep-seated envy and unease. We have to learn to appreciate the uniqueness of our own divine deposit — our personality and gifts — instead of coveting someone else's blessings. You may not know what they have to do to keep what they have. It is always wise to remember: "Everything that glitters didn't start off as gold."

The good news for those who feel as if they have permanently exempted themselves out of God's best blessings and for those who never feel quite adequate around people who seem more talented, is that *greater things are possible for you now in the place where God has positioned you.* This is a simple principle I want to plant within your psyche. You may not have to move across the country to start over again after you divorce your spouse. Maybe the greater life is in the acceptance of where you are. When you know that this is where you are supposed to be, you can fight for the marriage and experience greater life together instead of trying to create it apart. Often, God's greater purpose in any area of your life means giving up your false expectations of greatness in order to find the greater things God has called only you to do.

Simply stated, we carry false expectations of greatness. People think success is bling, rings, and things. People worship success because of power, money, and sexual attraction. We try to live into the world's notions of success and find ourselves hollow. It also means giving up on what others can do that you *wish* you could do, or what you *would* do if you had certain gifts that you frankly don't have or will never develop. No, you cannot sing, so why waste time daydreaming and coveting someone else's singing gift that you will never have?

Let's face facts: Most of us will never sing on a major national TV competition, so why would we waste valuable energy wishing for something we will not have? Or you may be under pressure to be successful like your family members, but you know God has called you to a different journey. I may wish to sing, but my family may wish for me to be a doctor or a lawyer. It takes courage to wrestle away from the bondage of other people's perception of us. When we give up how we look at success and embrace Christ's model of greatness — service, love, justice, and righteousness — we are liberated to be our very best selves.

Moving beyond thinking of 'good' as 'good enough' also requires embracing the limitations of your current life and then deciding to trust God completely and fully, to see yourself not as limited but as having what you need. Simply stated, it all starts where you are! You have everything you need. You have been gifted with every talent you will need. Stop seeing what you do not have and trust God enough to see that you have every resource you need to be God's best.

When we trace Elisha's journey, we see his ascendance to the position as senior prophet of Israel. When we get to II Kings 4, he is confronted with a problem that requires some examination.

One of the sons of the prophets has died, and his widow went to Elisha to pour out her heart. At the same time, Elisha heard of the death of a member of a band of preachers with which he was affiliated. His death was difficult because his wife was grieving heavily, but then she was in need of provisions.

When you read the story, it would appear that Elisha was very insensitive toward the woman's problem. There was a massive debt owed by her late husband, so a lien had been placed on her sons. The debt of the house was now upon the shoulders of her children. The debt collectors were positioned to sell these young male sons into servitude. Their mother was fighting to keep her family together.

Elisha asked her a serious and penetrating question, "What do you have in your house?"

This question of personal reflection and self-inventory is a fertile ground of exploration. I want to consider this 'house' metaphor and discuss the power of exploring what is in our own houses. If you would indulge me, I would like to use this 'house' to represent our community. Elisha suggests that we start fixing our problems and saving our families with what we are able do at home, through the resources that are already available to us in our 'house'. This may very well be the answer to the predicament of young men throughout our nation. While we have been waiting on the *House* of Congress — including the *House* of Representatives — or even the White *House* to fix our problems, maybe it is time we answered the prophetic question: What do we have in our house?

From a cultural perspective, perhaps part of the problem

and much of the solution is that we constantly look outside of our communities, to every other social and political agency and outlet, to fix the problems of genocidal warfare that suck young African-American men into the vacuum of the afterlife. We rarely take time to investigate what we might be able to offer as a means of solution — participation within the 'house'. What resources are in our communal 'houses' that can save our sons?

Too many churches have forsaken young people because they have tattoos and dress differently than our middle-class values. We have driven them out because they don't fit what we think should be seen in our 'house'. Churches have long been places that supported young people, institutions that saved the future of our children. We must offer programs and support that challenge and encourage our children. They are no longer safe in places where we send them. We have to do all we can as pastors and church 'house' leaders to see what is in our 'houses' and help save our children. What does your ministry or church have in the 'house' to save the children that have been charged to your care?

Parents, we have to check our houses and use what we have to save our children. We cannot merely blame other people and things for the condition of our children, but, rather, we must use what we have in the house to save our kids. We must go back to:

- Teaching respect;
- Developing their character;
- Showing them a functional model for marriage;
- Showing them how to be a responsible parent; and

- Teaching them the benefit of books instead of just reciting their favorite songs.

Parents, involve your child in a mentoring program. Expose them to the news instead of reruns of *106 & Park*. Are you teaching your sons how to dress for success? Are you teaching your sons how to talk to be understood? Are you teaching them what it means to be a young and intelligent Black man? Are you offering up anything in the 'house' to aide in the saving of your sons?

I will not deny the structural and systemic issues that constantly harass and oppress people of color and other marginalized people. We have an obligation to fight injustice and to confront all of the '-isms' that dehumanize people. But, we must also confront the lack of communal self-reflection. We cannot blame and critique other groups' responses to African-American manifestations of larger cultural and social issues without African-Americans as a community addressing them first. Quit using what you think you lack in the 'house' as your excuse for laziness and helplessness. Though you were given a bad hand, you can play the hand you have while ensuring that the next hand is dealt fairly.

The narrative in II Kings 4 suggests that a simple jar is not a bad place to start. After scouring the house for something to use to save her son, she finds a jar. A jar does not seem like an ingenious idea, but the widow is about to find out that all God needs is what she has to start with. All God needs is all you have. Here was this woman's problem. All she could focus on was what she didn't have. Elisha was more interested in her exception. She said, "I have nothing *except* a little oil." Her exception became the vehicle for an exceptional miracle. Sometimes we excuse ourselves from God's 'greater' in our lives because we believe we don't have enough for God to work with. Our exception becomes our excuse.

Maybe it's your lack of training, so you say you have nothing *except* a high school diploma. Maybe it's your lack of resources, so you say you have nothing *except* a few friends who are worse off than you. Maybe you feel you have insufficient experience, so you say you have nothing *except* a few years on this job. You let your 'except' keep you from realizing that what you have is more than enough for God.

In reality, using your 'except' as your excuse says more about what you think of God than of yourself. It suggests that you don't trust God or believe that God has the power to multiply your 'little' in order to cause it to be what you need it to be to do what it is He is calling you to do. The enemy wants to keep you from looking in your house to see what you already have and giving it to God to use. That's your place to start! A jar of oil seems ordinary, but it is a tool for the future freedom of not only the widow but also her children — setting her posterity free and ensuring a better tomorrow for her bloodline.

We should not despise our starting place, but we also need to discover the people we must see. It is about networking! I have found that life is about what you know *and* whom you know. Our lives are the sum of our relationships. The quality of our lives can be seen in the quality of our relationships. If you do not like the quality of your life, analyze the quality of your relationships and pray for discernment about why your relationships detract from your purpose. This is not a new idea, but I think it still applies. When the Lord wants to bless you, He will send you people. When the Devil wants to destroy you, he will send you people. Relationships and connections are so important in life.

Elisha tells the woman to go around to her neighbors and borrow jars from her neighbors. Watch what God does. People begin to help and assist her by giving her resources that she needs. She has people around her who have what it takes to help her in a time of need. God also puts a demand on resources she does not yet see, to multiply on her behalf, and a demand on people to help her who, up until now, have ignored her. All God needs her to do is have enough faith to use what she has to start with. When you begin to exercise faith in God, He will start putting demands on people to help you, even if you never knew they would help you.

There are two ingredients you will need if you are going to network: a plan and proper presentation. We discussed the power of planning in another chapter, but I want to talk about the importance of proper presentation. Elisha gave the woman a plan for her empowerment. He did not save the day, but he, in conjunction with the woman's effort, helped to create a new tomorrow for her family. The plan was to borrow jars from the neighbors, and in response to her faithful obedience to the prophetic instruction, God caused the oil to flow until everything she borrowed would be filled. Then she was to sell the oil and pay her debts.

She had a business plan given to her by God's representative. The execution of this plan was up to her. She had a plan, but she needed a solid presentation to her neighbors in order for them to lend her the jars. She could not go to her neighbors with a jacked-up attitude. She could not go to them with disjointed communication. She had to go to them communicating on such a level of faith and confidence that they would willingly give her their resources for a plan that did not make sense. Sometimes your presentation will cause people to sow into your life in ways that won't even make sense to them.

We often think that because we are nice, gifted, anointed, and sanctified, we can present our ideas and ourselves in any fashion to people and expect them to change the world. You can have more gifts than a Christmas tree and more olive oil than vinaigrette dressing, but if you do not present yourself in a way that people can receive, you will always find that the next level in your sights is out of your grasp.

Presentation is important. People judge us on how we look and carry ourselves. I am not promoting vanity, but too many people allow themselves to be viewed in ways that are unhelpful because they present themselves as someone to be misunderstood. When we speak, we have to present ourselves with the expectation of respect. How we dress our bodies, how we care for our transportation, and our display of respect for others demonstrates the way we present ourselves to the world.

The widow had a divine plan, and she also had a developed presentation for access to the higher life.

How will you present or represent yourselves? Maybe you have been stigmatized because of a negative presentation of yourself. Many of us have deep regrets over not presenting ourselves in the best light. This issue is more pervasive when we examine how social media has altered the way we present ourselves, especially for our young people. The Internet is forever. How our young people engage the world at their fingertips — private messages, Facebook status updates, Instagram pictures, SocialCam videos, and tweets — is now an issue of how they present themselves. Colleges and other institutions of higher learning now read Facebook posts and tweets to weed out students. YouTube is a medium for great good or great folly.

Our children and young people must realize that people judge your presentation, and one video, picture, post, or tweet can change their lives. The need for proper presentation goes beyond a plan, because many people plan a great life, but their problematic engagement with social media has altered how people see them, seemingly foiling the best-laid plans for a productive future. Make sure you are mindful of your presentation.

I love God because our 'except' helps provide us with the power to succeed. After the widow woman had done her networking, the text says the oil kept flowing until she had what she needed, not just to pay what she owed but also to keep on living. That is really where every family should be trying to be: Not just living from week to week to pay what you owe, but getting ahead so you have something to save, to sustain you. This is also a powerful principle when we consider how God allowed her situation to retrain her for future success.

She came to the prophet looking for help. She was about to lose her family, funds, and future. Instead of receiving a handout from God, her exception became a new avenue for future earnings. She came begging but left a business owner. She came looking for a miracle but *became* the miracle. The very thing she felt was inadequate became the avenue for a new future. The crises of her situation forced her to make her exception exceptional by discovering something about herself.

Do not curse your crisis. It is in the darkest of night that we are able to trace God's celestial hand pointing the way to a higher life. Crisis reveals our character. Crisis forces us to face our shortcomings and tap into our possibilities. We often pray for a life of ease, but an easy life can be a lazy life. A crisis forces us to take a critical assessment of our abilities and the capacities of the people around us. God will allow your crisis to shape and form you for a radiant and vibrant future.

Watch what God does! God used her little oil and an old jar as the beginning of a major overflow! It does not take much, even if you have to borrow it! God is not always looking for brand-new. God is more interested in our ability to *be* used. The woman was ready to be used and was willing to use anything that would help her in the pursuit of a better life.

The God who created something out of nothing can certainly create 'greater' out of little. God has a history of doing exceptional things with exceptions:

- Moses had nothing *except* his rod.
- Abraham had nothing *except* a wife who was barren.
- Jacob's exception was his limp.
- Gideon had nothing *except* three hundred men against a major army.
- David had to fight for his future with nothing *except* five smooth stones and a sling.
- Jesus had nobody *except* the doubting, duplicitous disciples.
- The little boy had nothing *except* five small loaves and two fish.

You may say, "That was then, but this is now." I hear you, and I want you to know that you are being called to the higher life and to leave 'good enough' in the past. You can do it no matter what your exception may be:

- Nothing *except* this inadequate job
- Nothing *except* a few dollars to pay some of my bills
- Nothing *except* me, myself, and I
- Nothing *except* some change in the sofa
- Nothing *except* a quarter of a tank of gas to get you through the work week

- Nothing *except* the clothes on your back as you start a new life

Do not let your 'except' become an excuse! Remember: It might not be enough to finish, but *it is always enough to start.* It's a good place to start. I know it seems like your resources will run out. It may feel like your sanity is going to run out. It may appear that hope is slipping through your curled fingers. I am here to remind you that your resources will not run out! They cannot run out until your overflow comes! You will have just enough until you walk into more than enough, if you work your plan and nail your presentation.

THE NECESSITY
OF AN ENEMY

A t the same time you are determining to ignite God's vision for your life and live a greater level of excellence than you have done in the past, the enemy is conspiring to kill it before you can ever start. If you get nothing else, get this: *Satan is the maestro of mediocrity*, and he will arrange all types of obstacles and forces in just the right manner to prevent the truth from settling in about how great you really are.

One of the ways he does this is through people. All around you are those who are still content with the ordinary. As a matter of fact, they spend a lot of time wondering why you are not satisfied with 'ordinary' anymore. Some of them will see this book in your hands and wonder why you are wasting your time with it. You have moved on to greater things, but they keep wishing that you would come back to the ordinary, because you were so much easier to deal with back then. You helped them to be comfortable with their laziness when you were lazy. You helped them be okay with their excuse-filled life when you offered excuses, as well.

They are the critics and eye-rollers who tell you that you're crazy to believe God can use you in a greater way. They treat you like you insulted them when you broke out of their well-defined expectations for your life. They are the friends who always point out your limitations rather than God's possibilities. It's that boss who would rather keep you busy doing grunt work instead of grooming you for promotion, all because of his own insecurities. It's that jealous co-worker who is trying to undermine you every chance he gets. You will always have people who are assigned to keeping you from fulfilling God's greater life for you. I want to suggest that they are a necessity for your maturity to handle life beyond 'good enough'.

I want to define 'enemy' as anybody who opposes or seeks to cause you to abort God's greater plan for your life. I know some of you may be thinking that using that word is a bit extreme, but if you do not see something that comes against God's purpose for your life as an enemy, then you will not do all that is required to conquer it before it conquers you. Anybody who is a threat to God's greater plan for your life and to you walking in 'greater' is an enemy. Some of you may consider this a crazy statement, but you will discover as you move through life and begin to ascend to new levels of potential and possibility that enemies are just as essential as friends. As a matter of fact, enemies are indicators to you that God is planning movement in your life and that transition is right around the corner.

When you read the Word of God, you will discover that whenever God's people, one or all, were about to move forward, they dealt with an enemy.

- It was Potiphar's wife, through her false accusations, who sent Joseph to prison, which ultimately set him up to be the prince.
- It was Pharaoh whose persecution served to multiply the Israelites into a mighty nation.
- It was Delilah and her seduction who caused Samson to renew his strength and multiply his influence by killing more in his second season than he did in his first.
- It was Goliath who took David from obscurity to notoriety.
- It was Nebuchadnezzar who turned three Hebrew slaves into Hebrew superstars.

It is not just important to see external people and threats as an enemy. Sometimes, we ourselves are often our worst enemy — think 'inner me' — to the plans God has for us. We are often the most recalcitrant and violent opposition to God's plans for our lives. Our habits, proclivities, and mindsets often war against the creative capacity that God desires to ignite in us. Our negative thinking, fits of anger, and selfishness are more deadly threats to the abundant life than anything we will face from others. We have to declare war on the 'inner me' or the enemy who seeks to dismantle God's blessings in our lives from the inside out.

I see this happening in a story found in II Kings 6:8. The King of Aram went to war against Israel, but something strange happened. Every time he tried to make a strategic move against the people of Israel, the armies of Israel anticipated it. Perplexed, the King of Aram asked about spies in the camp and was assured that there were none. However, they knew Israel had an aging prophet who, through the power of God, was able to tell the King of Israel every word the King of Aram whispered, even in his bedroom. When the King of Aram learned this, he decided that he needed to kill Elisha. So, under the thick cloak of midnight's darkness, they went down to Dothan, where Elisha was lodging.

Now, right away, I want to suggest something that is not expressly said in the text. One of my old homiletics professors, Dr. Henry Mitchell, used to tell us that sometimes best preaching is not in what is on the line but in what is *between* the lines.

The enemy showed one reason why they can never defeat you when you are walking in the Spirit: They make all of their calculations in the natural. The text has already told us that Elisha was able to hear everything the king said, even in his bedroom, which was how he was able to anticipate his every move. What makes him think that if God has allowed Elisha to hear every word, God would not let him hear about *this?*

One reason I believe Elisha didn't panic was because he already knew what was coming. When we live a life that is keenly attuned to the leading of God, we are often warned before problems come. In similar fashion to how God warned the prophet about the pending military raids, God will disturb our spirits and provide us with foreshadowing of future events.

Have you ever felt the Lord lead you home in a way different than your routine and you later discover that there was a major accident along your usual route? God is always warning and showing us how to live, but we have to be humble and open enough to hear God guide, whether with a whisper or an earthquake.

Early the next morning, the servant of Elisha woke up and saw the numerous and well-equipped armies of Aram surrounding the city where they slept. Unarmed, the servant grew increasingly afraid and ran to Elisha, asking the classic existential question we all know well when we are surrounded by adversity and enemies: *"What shall we do?"*

What opposition surrounds you and makes you fearful for the future?

Is it the critical people reminding you of all the ways you have blown it and of all the things you are or are not?

Is it your own inferiority and insecurity that keeps trying to remind you of the weaknesses inside of you?

Is it the sin that keeps tempting you?

Is it your past failures marching over your hopes and dreams?

Is it a lack of education and exposure to the outside world?

Is it a criminal record that people will not see beyond?

Is it years seemingly wasted in drug abuse, aggressive alcohol consumption, and uncontrolled sexual gratification?

It is the enemy's job to create circumstances around you that challenge the faith inside you. The enemy cannot destroy you, but it will provide all the tools for you to destroy yourself.

He does not have the power or authority to take you out, but he will provoke and make problems for you until self-destruction seems like the only option available.

The enemy will allow certain memories to loop in the processor of your mind. These memories are not often ones of joy, but visions, actions, and words that have scarred your soul and marred your heart. We cannot allow the replaying of the negative to provoke us to destroy the positive. If you have made a mistake, own it and move forward. Things may have happened to you that were unconscionable and sad, but you are still alive and you cannot let the opposition from the enemy make you so fearful that you refuse to take the next step.

How do you handle life when all you can see is your opposition and not your opportunities? Sometimes, the greater life seems harder to attain not only because of the opposition but because of those with whom we surround ourselves. If you are going to do what God has called you to do, you have to intentionally bring people into your life whom He wants you to, and put out the ones who subtract from your potential. The people who have significant input in your life will shape who you will become and what you will do, so choosing them carefully would be wise.

The Bible tells us that bad company corrupts good morals. The old saying still rings true, "Birds of a feather flock together." I see people who are constantly having their potential subtracted from them by people who do not make any positive additions to their life. Many people pray for more resources, like money, but human resources and relationships are far more valuable, because the circle of friends you have are a sneak preview into your future. If you are always the smartest, most dependable, and most responsible person in your group, then you may need to diversify your friendships. If you are the standard bearer, then how do you grow? Who feeds you? Our human resources and relationships show us who we are, where we are going, and in what shape we will be in when we arrive where we are headed.

Let me give you a way to identify the people you need to put out of your life, either for a season or altogether. Ask these questions:

- Who in my life leads me to attitudes or actions outside of what God prescribes for me in His Word?
- Who leaves me drained rather than empowered after a talk or encounter?
- Who keeps me thinking smaller rather than helping me dream bigger?
- Who constantly asserts that what I am attempting to do or be *will not work?*
- Who provides opportunities for my advancement and development?
- Who finds pleasure in directing me away from what God desires for me?
- Who encourages me to compromise my integrity for momentary thrills?

People who fit as answer to any of those questions need to have *limited access* to your space, or, if you cannot rid yourself of them, do what Elisha did in the text. Elisha prayed for his servant to see what he saw, which caused him to see what God had sent. He prayed for his servant to see what God already had in place. He prayed that God would take his servant's eyes off the natural resistance and let him see the spiritual reality. Elisha was saying that in order for us to work and walk together, his servant needed to see what he saw so they could both trust God.

There is a pertinent leadership principle here. Leaders must always be aware of how the people around them see the world, because if they see the same thing as the leader, they can work to the same outcome. Instead of being frustrated by those with whom you work and their lack of vision, you must work to increase their vision capacity. The servant, seeing the same thing as the prophet, kept his fear away because his leader's boldness transferred to the servant, because the leader was invested in how other people see.

It is not a wonder why Jesus, seeking to heal a blind man, spat in his eyes and asked him, "What do you see, now?" The healing of the man's blindness was a demonstration of the healing of the *spiritual* blindness that was needed for the disciples. You cannot lead people who cannot see what you see. Help them see the big picture. Help them see God in the midst of the most challenging predicaments.

You need people around you who can see what God has already placed at your disposal. You need friends who can see with the eyes of faith. To know what God has provided, you need friends who see beyond the natural and into the Spirit. It is not important that the people around you do not see the opposition;

it is important that they put their vision into perspective through faith. When you walk with the eyes of faith, you see something besides what your natural eyes can see.

Now, understand the delivery of the text in II Kings 6:17. The servant saw all of this *around* Elisha. The human opposition was all around the city, but the armies of the Lord were all *around* Elisha. The enemy could not get to Elisha without coming through the invisible but very real army of the Lord.

Often, our enemies seek to overtake us, but I want to remind you that our foes' efforts are futile. II Kings 6:18 describes Elisha's prayer concerning the opposition they faced. Notice the response to the prayer and the wording of the text in 6:19 to see what appears to be a contradiction. He prays for God to strike them blind; then he tells the *blind* armies to *follow* him. How do they follow him if they are blind? It is obvious that the armies aren't in total blindness, because how else would they be able to follow Elisha?

God said to me, "They could see but could not comprehend. They could see but could not understand." That's what God will do to your enemies. They can see you but can't comprehend what is going on with you. They will see you but can't get to you or near you. What a powerful thought. They can see you on the job but can't stop you from going for a promotion. They can see you in the church but can't stop you from working in the ministry.

Enemies can see what God is doing in your life but cannot perceive what is happening. It is almost as if these enemies are watching a movie in another language. They can see what is happening and make out some basic features, but they do not perceive the depths that God is working at in order to make you better and lift you into the higher life. People may see you driving a new car but not understand how God worked it out in your favor. People may see you being elevated but not see God's invisible hand going before you, making ways and opening doors. When people tell half the story, let them. Unless they can see what you see and stand where you stand, they will not understand what you have to do and what you are able to see. Do not misjudge the scope of your heavenly help because you are more focused on the opposition instead of on the opportunity. While they think they are getting you, God is really getting them.

I want to impress upon you that your readiness to move beyond just being good enough and into 'greater' will be seen in your maturity toward your enemy. You know you have matured when you stand ready to bless the people who tried to kill you. I know this seems oxymoronic, but how we treat our enemies demonstrates a change in us. I know it seems strange, but when we extend kindness to those who have harmed us, we signal to God that we have made peace with our past and are ready to leave the previous hurts and experiences behind us.

Our enemies may have done some inexplicable and deplorable things to us. However, the test of our maturity is not in how badly we treat our enemies but in how well we treat them. Anyone can be mean and hateful to someone who has been mean and hateful to them. It does not take increased spiritual maturity to curse out someone who cursed you out. No! Conversely, it doesn't take maturity to like the people who already like you. It is in our forgiveness of our enemies and our willingness to move out of the past that we show God we are ready for greater.

Do you want God's best? Do you want to leave the painful pits of past problems? If so, demonstrate to God that you are ready for the higher life by treating those with whom you have been at odds with respect and care. You may say, "You do not know what that person did to me." I agree with you. I do not know how deep was the pain or how traumatic the event. I do know this: When we open our eyes to what God will do for us in spite of them or even *through* what they did to us, it shrinks the size of our issue with the enemy.

This is precisely what Elisha did. He and his servant were able to subdue the hostile forces without violence, but with kindness. Elisha told the conglomeration of Israelite kings to provide a feast for the enemy. The kings were probably confused; the man of God said to provide a feast for someone who had come to hurt them? The prophet said to avoid being violent. Bless them! Provide for their needs!

After they were treated with respect, they backed off! The profundity in that simplicity is amazing to me. As the old saying goes, "Kill them with kindness." As David said, God will prepare a table before you in the presence of your enemies, but sometimes, when the table is set, you should invite them to eat.

Watch how the story concludes. The opposing forces never attacked Israel again. After they were treated graciously, they backed off. *How you react will determine how they respond.* If you love them, they have to back off. Have you ever considered that the Bible says God will make your enemies your footstool? A footstool is not just a piece of furniture to place your feet on; it is a practical piece of furniture that allows you to grab something on a higher level that you would not have been high enough to reach. God says that when enemies come against you, if you will embrace the mature life in Christ, God will use them and what they attempted to do to you as a step up to grab something on a higher level than you've ever been. Remember: The bigger the enemy, the bigger the footstool.

Enemies are just necessary to the climb.

TOO GREAT FOR YOUR OWN GOOD

I am an avid sports fan. My love of sports is deeper than the mere athletic feats of talented people. Watching highlights on ESPN and other sports networks provides daily visual reminders of how great some athletes are. Have you ever tried to dunk a basketball on a ten-foot basketball rim? Have you ever tried to throw a 100 mph fastball? What was your fastest time in the three-legged sack race at your fourth grade field day? These simple questions and their honest answers remind us that we watch greatness every time Kobe dunks or shoots a pure jump shot off of one leg while falling back and every time Usain Bolt strides down the Olympic track with the ease and speed of a gazelle.

Recently, I read an intriguing article about Tiger Woods. He schooled the entire field at the Bridgestone golf tournament. For those unaware of what 'schooling' may be, imagine being so great at what you do that people consider watching you engage your craft as a learning lesson in textbook execution; you are so great that you are teaching others how to be better while beating them at what they do. As other media outlets discussed his legacy, dominance, and wealth, one thing that has come up over and over has been his very public meltdown after poor choices he has made in his marriage.

The best perspectives of this public meltdown have come from the great Tiger himself. He talks very candidly about the firm grip and extensive power of pride. There is no question about his greatness, as evidenced by his numerous wins and constant positioning at the top of golf leaderboards around the globe, but he is just another example in a long line of people who had their greatness sabotaged because of self-centered pride.

Pride is the subtle but ever intensifying smell that cannot be covered with Givenchy or Bath and Body Works spray mist. Someone has said that pride is the hidden cancer that gnaws away at your insides. Pride is subtle; it kills with grand gestures or in small subtractions. Pride places the inner life in crisis because it hides in honest emotions and actions, and it slowly corrupts or quickly overtakes our motives. It lurks in the shadows of our victories and seeks to have its presence validated at every opportunity. Its secrecy is what makes it so lethal.

When you read James 4:6, you will discover, "Pride is the disposition of the heart that brings opposition from God." *Why?* Because pride is rooted in self-centeredness, and you can't be God-centered and self-centered at the same time. God has made it abundantly clear that He does not and will not share top spot with anything or anyone.

God is calling every one of us to come up higher, live with a sense of purpose, and to rest in the Divine plan. This book, up to this point, has explored the struggles and sacrifices it will take to really live a life of excellence. What I want to suggest in this chapter is that the greater we become in God, the less about *us* our lives should become. You do not build true greatness by adding self-esteem, *but by subtracting self-reliance.*

I know this may seem strange and even outlandish. Worldly greatness — standards for greatness that our culture celebrates — is based upon doing things for yourself, looking out for yourself, and celebrating yourself for doing what you want to do. The prefix 'self-' demonstrates that the origin of and motivation for your efforts is started in your own will and ends in your own glorification. Greatness is not about the constant attention we bring to our wallet, our palatial domicile, or to our wardrobe. It is manifest when we learn to take 'self' out of the source and beginning of our efforts. When we learn to prioritize God and minimize our own selfish and egotistical aims, we can really become great. Pride is a parade of flesh that seeks to live the divine life with earthly tools. Take your 'self' out of your success and watch God open doors and make ways on your behalf!

The higher you rise in God, the lower you will be willing to go in service. You will realize more and more that the purpose of living beyond just 'good enough' is not to bring attention to yourself. It is to bring glory and honor to the One who is and will always be greater. The more God does for me, the more I realize that I did not take myself as high as I am and that

I cannot keep myself there or advance myself. My complete success is resting in the plan of God and the position of my heart toward God.

If I am doing great things in order to be seen as great in the eyes of people, there is a limit to what I will do and where I will go. Why? Because we assign greatness to a look and not a lifestyle. "If I pick up trash off of the ground, how will I look?" Other people may say, "I cannot drive around in that type of car because that does not look successful." The purpose of the greater life is not to make us greater or make us *look* greater, but to show our God as greater. If the Lord can use you and I, God can use anybody!

In dealing with pride, can I tell you what I have discovered? I have discovered that from time to time, God has to bring something into our lives to help us realize that we are not as great as we think we are. God allows challenges in our lives that push us beyond our natural ability. Have you had a problem that no connection to powerful people or an infinite source of riches could help? Have you struggled with a crisis that it seems like no one else can help with or offer meaningful advice? God will allow certain situations to occur to arrest our wavering attention and shock our overconfident postures by reminding us that we have clay feet. We are human. We fail. We are not God.

God confronts our pride with challenges beyond our ability to fix, in order to position us for the greater life. God is so invested in us that He will, at times, allow painful things to happen to keep us from being too proud. *God will allow us to struggle to keep us coming back to the huddle.* God is so powerful that my problems are used for his glory and my growth. I do not want pride to keep me away from God and the greater life. I am glad that my problems force me to come back to the huddle of my local church body, friends who care, and a God who loves us.

Pride can keep you from the greater life when it convinces you that you are already great or that you are the source of your own greatness. I want to make a clear distinction between confidence and arrogance. We are to possess confidence but avoid arrogance. The similarity between confidence and arrogance are rooted in the assurance that you have talent.

For example, you can 'do some hair'. You have tremendous skills and technique in taking people's hair issues and turning them into sources of pride. Everyone tells you, "Girl, you know you can do some hair." In fact, you are so gifted at doing hair that you can do it in a shop or in your kitchen. You can fry, dye, and lay it to the side. The difference is that arrogance mistakes the source as the self, while confidence confirms that the source of all of your talent and greatness is found in God. Arrogant folks believe that they are the reason for their ability. Confident folks say, "I know what I am able to do, but I am only able to do it because God is the source of it all!" So when you do hair, do it to the glory of God. When you wash and wrap a woman's head, give God the glory. When you wash someone's head in the washbowl, scratch their scalp to the power and glory of Almighty God!

I am convinced that we have confused some of these popular terms. Another such term is 'humility'. It doesn't mean being a human kickball for the recreation of your co-workers or a punching bag for your spouse. The devil is a liar. You do not have to put yourself down and appraise your worth as lower than a duck's footprint. That's not humility. That is dangerous and misguided low self-esteem. The Bible tells us that we are ". . . the head and not the tail." The Bible tells us that we were made ". . . a little lower than the angels." The Bible says we are ". . . above, not beneath." Humility is about the unwavering recognition that God has given me what I have, taught me what I know, and will lead me where I need to go. Humility says that I know there may be people with more talent than I have, but God can take what I have and allow me to do what others cannot do. Have confidence . . . in God!

In II Kings 5, we meet a man by the name of Naaman. He was a great man, a national hero who was known for his courage. His claim to fame was that he had engineered victory for his country, Aram. God had used him even though he was not an Israelite. He was so great that even as a non-Israelite, an outsider, he was recognized beyond his circles of influence as a great man. One of the things we are going to discover with Naaman is that *people who are great often have even greater needs*. The more gifted you are, the more problematic you may become without proper perspective.

Naaman is one of those persons who has so much going for them that when you see how low their self-esteem is, you cannot figure out why they are so insecure. Do you know someone like that? They have more gifts than a Christmas tree but act like they have nothing to offer the world or anything to live for. It's compelling to try to figure out what in the world would make him insecure with all that he had going for him. His pride was really a mask for deep-seated insecurity.

Our insecurities often manifest as arrogance. We act like we are better than people because we really see ourselves lower and less worthy than them. You just purchased your first German luxury vehicle and now you have lost touch with those rainy days when you stood waiting on a bus to take you to work. *We assume we are better than others because of what we have, when we really feel deficient at our core.*

He is an example of the reality that you can be a great person who keeps looking for something greater, because in spite of all of the great things you possess, you still feel lesser. In other words, you can have all the external signs of greatness but yearn for something more or think less of yourself than your external suggests. You can have the trappings of success and be trapped by that very same success. Then you begin trying to keep an image that your economy can't afford, trying to impress people who will never like you, to be invited places where you do not even feel comfortable.

Naaman had two problems that tried to keep him from being the great person his great accomplishments said he should be. His first problem was that he had leprosy, a disease that affected not only the skin, but the mind, as well. It was a social and physical malady. It was a terrible prognosis. Leprosy would cause discoloration and rotting of the skin, open sores, and puss-filled wounds. It was an ugly and painful way to exist. Lepers, because of the highly-contagious nature of their disease, were forced to live on colonies with other lepers. They were isolated from people, places, and the potential for a better life. So dehumanizing and socially immobilizing was leprosy in the ancient world that those who had it were required to shout from long distances, "Unclean!" when non-lepers were in proximity.

He was a man of influence with an affliction. It disfigured him, made him a social plague. He was quarantined and forced to die alone. The negativity of it all is really seen in the writer's language in describing Naaman. He lists all of Naaman's great qualities and then negates them all with a contravening conjunction that gives a subordinating feeling: 'but'. Let me suggest a few things about this.

God does not need you to be perfect in order for you to walk in purpose. God does not need you to be an honor roll student in order for you to be utilized in the manifestation of the Kingdom of God. God does not need a perfect person, but God definitely needs a willing person. God is not looking for perfection; God is looking for submission.

Notice that Naaman had leprosy but did not live in a lepers' colony. He lived in a palace where he had no business being able to live. This one thing should have disqualified him from living like he was living, yet there he was, living differently and better than this one thing meant he should have been. Much like Naaman, when we reflect on the 'but' that would have negated our very presence, we realize that things do not have to be as blessed as they are. You made some mistakes and things did not go well. You did what you should not have done and said what you should not have said, but you are still where you are. Something bad happened to you as a child, but look at you now. You have a family and a future. God gave Naaman more than he deserved, and he was able to enjoy success with an issue that would have disqualified him from the greater life.

Naaman's problem was not his leprosy. Naaman's problem was his view of himself with the leprosy. Your problem is not the one thing that is wrong with you; your problem could be how you see and think about yourself with your issue. We have often given so much power to our problem that we do not even feel like a person anymore. He was so consumed by the one thing that was obviously wrong that he could not celebrate all the things that were right.

Let's be honest: We all have or have had that one thing that should have disqualified us. All of us can think of one thing that should have kept us away from our purpose, the plans of God, and the blessings of our connection to Christ. I have to remind myself, and I want to remind you, to think and thank God for all of the things that your problem did not keep you from experiencing. People said you would never have a family and give birth because of reproductive issues, but every time you hold your child, you can think and thank God for how your problem did not disqualify you. Whenever you think about your time in foster care or your bid in prison, it depresses you. You ought to thank God that your problem did not keep you from learning a trade and making something out of the life

God gave you. The one thing that society says is wrong with you will not keep God from using you!

If we let him, the enemy can get us so focused on that one thing that we miss out on and mess up all the great things that God is doing in spite of us, for us, and through us. Anyone can celebrate what God is doing when things are perfect, but a perfect God can take an imperfect me and get the glory! *Make your embarrassment your empowerment!*

Here is what the enemy does. He enlarges and illuminates your feelings of inferiority and insecurity by causing you to give too much weight to what others think about your one flaw. The enemy is crafty and clever, because we end up focusing so much on how we think other people perceive our issue that we become enslaved to what we think people think. We are so engrossed in what our family, friends, and even foes think about our one flaw that we are frozen in the 'paralysis of analysis'. We are so trapped in the deep analysis of our issue that we are unable to move.

Do not let your one flaw freeze you, because we all have our 'but' that travels with us along the journey of purpose. Moses' 'but' was that he was a stutterer. Samuel's 'but' was that he was called as a little boy. Isaiah was a man of impure and unclean lips. Paul's 'but' consisted of his thorn in an uncomfortable place — his flesh. We all have a 'but' somewhere.

Naaman did not write II Kings; therefore, he did not write this description of himself. Somebody else wrote the description. This is the chronicler's descriptive opinion of Namaan. He did not write this about himself, and he did not add the 'but' in the text. Someone observing his condition described him based on their opinion of his condition. The description of Naaman would have had the same facts with a different conjunction: 'and'. The writer of the text, by using 'but' instead of 'and', was making a statement: Whatever Naaman's strengths were, they were overturned by what was wrong with him.

Everyone is entitled to his or her opinion of you and what you do. The fact that they have an opinion about your 'but' is not your problem, because it's their opinion. What will keep you above the opinions and definitions others have about you is how *you* describe them. I do not have to change the facts of my life, but I can change the conjunction. They say it with a 'but'; I say it with an 'and'. "My name is Mrs. Do Better *and* I am divorced." "My name is Mr. Work Harder *and* I went to prison." It is about how you tell your story! Tell your story with an 'and'. Do not allow people to shape your perspective of yourself. When they come to you with a 'but', change it to an 'and'! We need to get an 'and' attitude. The word 'and' will liberate you, because 'and' signals an attitude adjustment and a refusal to let your deficiency be defined by the opinions of others.

Another promising principle we see in Naaman's life is that you must keep yourself small through your daily interactions with people around you. Stay a 'people person', or become a 'people person', because God sends blessings through people. Notice the slave girl in this text has an affection and affinity for Naaman, to the extent that she longs to see him better. That only happens because of how he operates around her and treats her. He has obviously treated her in such a way that an affinity grew toward him from someone you would never think had anything to offer him. Naaman's greatness on a daily level and his engagement with people considered 'lesser' than him was paying dividends. His greatness in terms of character and integrity created a bond with people considered not as great as him, to help him be great. Do not miss this!

Often, we dismiss and distain people who we feel we do not need. Being great as a parent, leader, coach, pastor, business owner, and friend is based on how you treat people and how they treat you. Naaman's servant is so passionate about his healing that she is willing to not only observe the problem but also offer a possible solution. The saying is true, "Treat everybody right, because you never know who will have to bring you cold water on a hot day." Treat people right! Your blessing may come through people who you never would imagine could bless you. We have to mature beyond superficial relationships. If our blessings come through people, we have to ensure that we cultivate relationships with people so God's blessings can flow. You may be entertaining angels or potential blessings and not even know it.

Although Naaman was the model of greatness, he was open to advice from someone seemingly 'beneath' him. He was the man, the leader, listened to but also willing to listen. *Don't let your pride cause you to turn a deaf ear to people who are only trying to bless you.* I'm not suggesting that everybody is worth listening to, but if you have an established relationship, you ought to know that their words come from a good place. Insecure people always get defensive when anybody tries to offer them anything that can help them. Yes, you may be the boss on the job, but your assistant knows how the office really works. You may be a pastor, but a staff member may have an idea that you have not thought of. God can use anyone to do anything, so just because you think that the person may be small does not mean they do not have something big to offer you and share with the world! Sometimes we need to stop talking and start listening! Listen to what the Spirit is saying, and it may come through people you have overlooked.

Naaman heard about the prophet Elisha from the handmaiden and felt it was worth an attempt to see what God could do through this person. Naaman went to the house of Elisha, who refused to indulge Naaman's expectations of healing. Instead, he sent him away with a simple instruction: To dip in the muddy Jordan River seven times. All he had to do was as he had been instructed, and he would be healed. He had received thousands of orders in his life. It would seem that after many years of suffering, Naaman might finally resume a regular life, because he knew how to follow instructions.

Now, you would think that Naaman would go away rejoicing that a cure had been offered. God was not working on his leprosy as much as on his pride. God wanted to see if Naaman would be able to follow an instruction to do something that he thought was beneath him. God wanted to see if Naaman, the military leader of a mighty nation, would humble himself to listen to a strange prophet in a distant land, to dip in water that seemed inferior to the waters of his homeland, not once but seven times.

An invitation to the life that goes beyond the good life can sometimes begin when God asks us to do something we do not want to do. Sometimes, God will ask you to do the one thing you don't want to do. "I will love everybody, except that person." "I will forgive anything, except that one thing." "I will help any person but her." Get off that high horse and do what God says!

Maturity and freedom in Christ are connected to obedience in areas of our lives where we want to resist God and the developmental process. We all have areas where we struggle to surrender to the Lordship of Christ. We want to pick and choose the domain where God reigns in us. God is developing us through our attention and commitment to obedience. We can never arrive where God wants us to be by taking our own path to get there.

You won't recognize your pride until God asks you to do a humbling thing. *You have to learn how to immediately obey specific instructions.* God can use you in greater ways when you obey simple instructions. The issue was not the river water but obedience to God. The point was, "Naaman, if you can just be obedient to the Word of God, *he can bless you even through dirty water.*" Don't miss the point. The point is not about the water. The point is about trusting in the sovereign power of God. When you get caught up in the tricks and trappings of religion — looking for God to bless you however you think God will do it — you will always look for tricks to bless you.

There are many well-intentioned believers who have assumed that the healing and maturity they seek can be found in tricks and tricky behavior. Instead of being obedient, we try to trick God into blessing us by giving money (sowing seeds). We listen to tricky preachers who are more consumed with consumption than by the Holy Spirit. Church is not a magic show, and the preacher is not David Copperfield. The commercial says it all: "Silly rabbit, tricks are for kids!" We cannot move up without obedience to the small things!

All God needs is your obedience, and then even the dirty water can't stop the healing, because you will be healed of pride. Can you imagine dirty, contaminated water? God stopped its contamination from getting in the sores and infecting Naaman. Has God ever blessed you when you were in dirty waters? What is your Jordan River, and what keeps you from wanting to dip in it? Who do you struggle to forgive? Is it the dirty water of your addictions? Do you not want to dip in the river of your dirty finances? Who do you need to love? Which co-worker do you need to help? To whom do you need to apologize? What lies have you told that you need to apologize for? What child do you need to support, who is not being taken care of properly? What sin do you need to give up? What relationship do you need to quit? No tricks. Just dip.

When Naaman finally went into the Jordan, he was not just lowering his body but also his pride. Do not miss the fact that he dipped seven times. One dip would have been an accident, but a constant self-immersion demonstrated not only to himself but also to everyone associated with him that a great person is great because they are willing to lower themselves in obedience to be raised in greatness.

I'M DISAPPOINTED WITH GOD

In the earlier chapters, we have been walking through the life of the prophet Elisha, and we have discovered that Elisha was a man who dared to believe in the greater life. He not only believed in it, but he also took the sacrificial steps necessary to walk in it.

- He burned his plows, which were a part of his past stable life condition. He decided that he did not want to live his life in the suitable or 'good enough'. He burned his plows however, because he knew that along the way to 'greater' everyone has seasons and moments in which they wonder if the struggle is worth it and are tempted to go back and settle into what has always been comfortable and safe. He showed us that the only way to insure that you do not go back is to make sure that you have nothing to go back to.

- We have learned along the way that part of living the life that refuses to let 'good' be 'good enough' is imparting that greater life into the lives of others so that they can experience the greater life, as well. We have watched Elisha challenge a nation to dig ditches in advance of the outpouring of God, showing that you have to learn how to plan your work and then work your plan in anticipation of the manifested miracle you believe will come.

- We then saw him imparting this greater life to a single mother who was having issues with her finances, family, and her future. God taught her that the life beyond 'good' begins by looking inside your own home and using what God has placed at your disposal, no matter how insignificant it might appear.

We have also discovered that this journey of commitment to living the life beyond 'good enough' is marked with setbacks and real suffering. Sometimes, as your faith gets stronger, your situation seems to get worse. Sometimes you pray in great faith, act in obedience, and the miracle still doesn't come. What happens when the ditch is dug but the rain doesn't come? What do you do if you gather all of the jars and the oil doesn't flow? Sometimes, you have done everything you know to do and have been *told* to do, and you end up with a sense of disappointment in this season with God. It is hard to handle a deep sense of sadness when God seemingly lets us down.

It can feel like prayer is feeble, fickle, and foolish. You can end up feeling like God has failed you, or that faith is not a real force. You did everything to make your marriage work, but your spouse left you anyway. You prayed to be healed, but the doctors couldn't get rid of the tumor. You launched out in faith and started a new business venture, trusting that it was a God move, but then it failed and you were sent back to square one. You did all you were supposed to do concerning your finances but were still in need of a miracle, and you prayed believing that God would intervene, only to have the house foreclosed on or the car repossessed. You sowed seeds of faith on behalf of your child, and yet she still ended up pregnant and unwed.

Let me suggest to you that suffering and those times where you are confounded by God's lack of or unexpected response are not to be seen as evidence that God is not with you or did not hear your prayer. Discouragement and frustration are often not signs of being on the wrong path but on the right one.

I read this phrase somewhere and it blessed me: *God may not always answer your prayers, but He never wastes our faith.* When you have the faith to persevere and trust, to believe through the droughts of unanswered prayer, there is a certain reward for it. All of us have experienced unanswered prayers, but in the economy of God, no one's faith is ever wasted. Not one word is unusable and unhelpful in the services of God and the maturation of our lives. If God promised, God will deliver. If you don't get anything else, get this: God is working on our behalf even when our prayers do not seem to be working at all. God is working even when the gears of our lives feel stuck.

The next phase of Elisha's journey brings us into a direct confrontation with a woman who is frustrated and disappointed with God. She is referred to as 'the Shunammite woman', known only by her birthplace. It is interesting to me that it would appear that her life had been just fine until God got involved. I can see you nodding; you've been there, when life seemed to be amazingly mediocre but stable. Then, all of a sudden, you let God in and things go south. God is the spoon that mixes things up in our lives, agitating and stirring the hopes, dreams, and plans that sank to the bottoms of our souls and is forcing them to the top.

She was a woman of great wealth, but even greater generosity. Whenever Elisha's ministry brought him to or near her hometown, she insisted on providing hospitality to him. She had developed a tender spot for the man of God and went to her husband about the possibility of building a room onto their house just for him. They built the room, and it became Elisha's home when in that region.

One day, Elisha decided that he wanted to show kindness to the woman and her husband for being so kind to him. He called his servant to go and get the woman and asked her if he could do anything for her. She, in her humility, modesty, and suppressed level of expectation about the dream she kept in the diary of her heart, said that she needed nothing from him.

I have noticed that many of us, when faced with opportunities to receive from God, often ignore the sore and tender spots on our hearts, those places where we have tried to conceive a new reality but have failed in the process. The Shunammite woman's desire was not shared from her own lips but relayed to the prophet by his servant, who informed Elisha that the woman had sought to conceive a child but had been unsuccessful.

Yes, she proves to us that you can have almost everything, but what you lack is often the one thing you desire the most. Notice that she had everything a person could ask for, except the thing that would bring her the deepest joy — a child. It is possible to love God, be successful, but still have a longing that is hidden because of past disappointment. The area that she desired to be fruitful in was unfruitful. Her life was a lush orchard, but the most beautiful tree was perpetually barren, waving to passing birds with limp limbs and seeking to extract moisture from unresponsive earth. There was social shame attached to barrenness; her culture saw fruitlessness of the womb as a curse. She had both success and shame. She was in a perplexing bind of frustration. She was in the midst of fruitfulness and faithfulness but still holding her dreams close to her aching heart.

Elisha told the woman that by that time next year, she, in her advanced age, would give birth to a child. This was obviously a painful subject for her, and her response was to beg him not to tease her. She felt so futile in her infertility that she saw the promise as a cruel joke at her expense. She saw God's invitation as a painful reminder of her failure. She was no different than we can be when faced with the promise and prospect of 'greater'. We get so handcuffed to hopelessness as a result of our history that the thought of producing starts to sound like a cruel joke.

When you have lived with 'lesser' long enough, the possibility of 'greater' can seem like a joke. Have you ever had to believe against the backdrop of previously unfulfilled desires? What could convince you that God's plan for you could be greater than anything you have ever experienced or imagined when your dreams heretofore have been unfulfilled?

When we pray for something and it doesn't happen, we tend to believe that our faith was wasted. It takes a deeper level of faith to continue believing when your life has been defined by unfulfilled desires. Anyone can believe that God *can* when God already *has,* but it takes a mature believer to survey all that God has done in other areas of life and conclude that if God made those other areas of my life fruitful, then this one is coming around soon!

II Kings 4:17 becomes one of my first principles from this story on reaching for the life that is beyond being satisfied with 'good'. You have to possess within yourself an *influential* faith. You have to have the kind of faith that is able to lean on and impress upon others until they begin to believe like you do. It is a seemingly mundane part of the story, but it is key.

In that verse, she conceived a child. This is a miracle in itself. After years of nothing, she finally conceived. Now, remember, her husband did not hear Elisha's prophetic declaration, but he had to have been involved for the conception to occur. It is obvious that they had been trying with no results in the past, and her husband was up in age where it seemed next to impossible. His wife had to be the one to relay the message from Elisha, which means that her faith had to be influential enough to convince her husband, beyond all of his doubts, to give it one last try.

Sometimes, to get into the life that moves you beyond 'the good life', you have to have such a faith that you are able to lift others up to your level of faith and make them believe that what you want to create is possible. If you do not possess an influential faith, then you are not ready for the greater things of God.

Every parent has to have this influential faith. You have to be able to influence your children's faith by telling them they can be anything they want when they think they will become another statistic. You have to convince your child that they can learn and succeed. You may have to convince your daughter that her body is a temple of the Holy Spirit and that she has to be mindful of whom she is with and where she goes. You have to convince your child that the fear of the Lord is the beginning of wisdom. You have to have the influential faith that not only shifts their minds but their destinies.

Your spouse needs to have this influential faith. Influential faith looks the other spouse in the eye and lets them know that the marriage will survive and come out stronger. Influential faith helps to demonstrate to a spouse that the financial challenges will not last forever. Influential faith loves a partner into wholeness and never shatters them into pieces. Influential faith can take you from the divorce court to another honeymoon!

Every leader has to have this influential faith. If you do not have influential faith, you need to seriously consider why and how you lead people. Influential faith separates the wanderers from those who are taking the path to destiny. We must have influential faith to show people what eyes cannot see. If your faith is influential, the future is not a dream; it is tangible and people will believe it. Is your faith influential? Do you have the faith to lead people into the higher life?

The Shunammite woman's son, a child of destiny, heartbreak, and heart's joy, became sick and died. I don't know about you, but I would rather it had never happened than for it to happen only to be suddenly snatched from my weak and frail grasp. Lord, why would you let me get so close to what I have always wanted and then take it away as if I never had it? Lord, why did you wake up something in me that you have now rocked back to sleep?

Have you ever felt that way? Maybe you did when your marriage ended after promising yourself that you would not ever get married anyway. It could be the ending of a job that was supposed to take you into retirement. I would rather have been left alone than have my desired companionship only for a season. Many of us struggle because we allow one setback to destroy our perspective of God's plan for our lives.

Here is my next principle: We must have greater faith in God's greater plan. We cannot judge the scope of God's complete work in our lives from the disadvantaged position of disappointment. Disappointment and heartbreak are human emotions, but they, being emotions, can skew our perspective of ourselves and cause us to miss out on what God can do in a dead situation. We have to be careful of allowing the lenses of pain to change what and how we see. We cannot see the beginning from the end, but God can. We have to trust God's plan even when our eyes are too heavy with tears to allow clear sight and unclouded vision. A painful position can be a disadvantage if we do not keep the broader scope of God's plan before us.

Pain can shorten our ability to see the long-term. Pain stresses immediacy and the instant. Pain can push us to see comfort that is superficial, relationships that are unhealthy, and habits that are destructive. We have to feel pain, but we do not have to have painful perspectives. It may seem that time and prayers were wasted and the situation seems over, but God surprises us at every moment.

Maybe God allows certain situations to die because *the death of a situation can bring life to our faith.* Some of us have become so structured, planned, and logical that when God seeks to surprise us, we are not even around. Death, from the perspective of a Christian, is not a period; it is a comma. A period ends a sentence, but a comma lets us know that there is more to come. Just because something is dead does not mean it is over.

I dare you to look around and watch the comma that God is about to insert. Your dreams seemed to die when you could not afford college, but the lack of financial aid is a comma, not a period. The economic downturn has quickly turned your savings into loose change, but the recession was not a period; it was a comma. Some of us need to brush up on our punctuation and learn that after something seems to die, God can take a heavenly ink pen and place a comma where we thought everything was over. It is not over; it is still unfolding. No promise from God is ever dead.

This woman had this kind of faith. Remember: When you want others to participate and partner with you in faith, you cannot allow others to prohibit you with their lack of faith. The child she hid in her soul was lying cold in her arms. She faced the peculiar punctuation of life, between a comma and a period. She decided to trust that God had a comma waiting on her. She sought to gain agreement from the father, her husband. He had faith, but not strong enough to touch and agree with her. Isn't it interesting that the husband believed for the child against all odds, but couldn't believe for another miracle?

We often face issues and situations in which people who believed with us for the initial blessing are now unable to believe for the next miracle. Further, we are disappointed and dissuaded from belief in another miracle because of others' lack of enthusiasm. Never let your surroundings overpower the buoyancy of your faith. You may be carrying your lifeless dream, your decaying family, your soon-to-be-foreclosed-upon house, your car constantly needing repairs, or your calling that seems unresponsive, but just because others do not rush to believe with you does not mean that it is not important. Get up! Get serious! Do not allow other people's pain or limited thinking to keep you believing more in the problem than the problem-solver.

We know the story. She went to the man of God and laid her complaint at his feet. He did something very interesting:

He laid down on the boy and then put his mouth on the boy's mouth and breathed into him. It matters whom you let speak over you. You only want people putting their mouth on you who have what it takes to breathe life back into you. His servant tried using Elisha's staff to revive the boy, but that didn't work. It took Elisha putting his mouth on the boy and breathing life into him. It took Elisha breathing a fresh wind into his failed lungs. It took a new wind to reinvigorate the cessation of physical activity.

I realize that many of us are carrying dead things, but we carry those things to people who are dead themselves. These unhelpful people breathe the stale air of doubt and fear into our already dead situation. We need to look around in our lives and do a breath check. Who is bringing you fresh breath? Who celebrates the small things in your life? To whom can you bring your beloved dead thing and know something will happen? You need to ask God to connect you to people who have the faith to breathe life into you. Get off the respirator of artificial air and allow God to breathe into your life afresh.

It all happened because of the woman's faith to believe past unfulfilled dreams and dashed desires. Notice that Elisha kept going back to lie on the boy, and the boy started to get warm. When he felt warmth from the boy, he went back and repeated the process. He continued to repeat the process until the child sneezed and opened his eyes. It all happened in stages. He didn't come back all at once. There was no immediate full recovery. This recovery happened in stages. Elisha had to know how to celebrate progress.

As I come to the close of this book, that is a final thought I would like to leave you with. Learn how to celebrate your progress. Too many people sit around sulking because of all the things that are still not right. Starting right now, right here, I want you to start celebrating what is already better. There is something to be said for recognizing and celebrating progress. I hope that since you have been reading this book, there has been progress in some of the areas of your life where you know you have settled for being 'good'. See the progress as a sign that you are on the right road to discovering that 'good' is not 'good enough' and that 'better' is available.

CONCLUSION/RSVP

The introduction to this book is an invitation to the higher life. This book has attempted to provoke thought and inspire change so that the reader would be willing to imagine their world bigger, broader, and better than before.

From an etiquette standpoint, when someone sends you an invitation, often there is an option to RSVP — *"Répondez s'il vous plait."* In French, this means 'Please respond.'

This conclusion is an RSVP for the higher life. We have experienced the strength and vulnerability of Elisha and those who are instrumental to his journey. We have seen people disappointed with God, walking away from the mediocre, and preparing for the flood of God's blessings. Elisha received the cloak, the invitation to another level of power and prophecy, but his *response* was the key.

How will you respond to the enormous potential God has given you? What will you do to ensure that you properly respond to an invitation so big that God will talk about you to other people in order to bless you? It is bigger than where you have been and what you have done? Whatever you have seen, God is bigger. Whatever your routine, God is broader. How do you handle the opportunity to change your life and alter the trajectory of your family and friends? Simply — respond.

Give God your RSVP marked 'yes'. God is seeking to make you greater because the world needs your greatness. We are drowning in our own average behavior and subterranean issues of character, confidence, and consciousness. God has invited us to take it to the next level. What is your response? Will you join God in working at the next level? We need you! The world needs you! God desires to use you! Tell the Lord 'yes' and prepare for the radiance of life that helps you discover that while 'good' was nice, it's just not good enough.

Grace and Peace